Craft Hope

Craft Hope

Handmade Crafts for a Cause

Jade Sims

A Division of Sterling Publishing Co., Inc.
New York / London

Editor
KATHY SHELDON

Editorial Assistant
BETH SWEET

Art Director
KRISTI PFEFFER

Photography Director
DANA IRWIN

Junior Designer
CAROL MORSE

Art Assistant
BRADLEY NORRIS

Illustrator
ORRIN LUNDGREN

Principal Photographer
LYNNE HARTY

Cover Designer
PAMELA NORMAN

Library of Congress Cataloging-in-Publication Data

Sims, Jade.
  Craft hope : handmade crafts for a cause / Jade Sims. -- 1st ed.
    p. cm.
  Includes index.
  ISBN 978-1-60059-624-7 (pb-flexibound : alk. paper)
  1. Handicraft. I. Title.
  TT157.S5282 2010
  745.5--dc22

                        2010000447

10 9 8 7 6 5 4 3 2 1

First Edition

Published by Lark Crafts, A Division of
Sterling Publishing Co., Inc.
387 Park Avenue South, New York, NY 10016

Text © 2010, Jade Sims
Photography © 2010, Lark Crafts, A Division of Sterling Publishing Co., Inc., unless otherwise
specified
Illustrations © 2010, Lark Crafts, A Division of Sterling Publishing Co., Inc., unless otherwise
specified

Distributed in Canada by Sterling Publishing,
c/o Canadian Manda Group, 165 Dufferin Street
Toronto, Ontario, Canada M6K 3H6

Distributed in the United Kingdom by GMC Distribution Services,
Castle Place, 166 High Street, Lewes, East Sussex, England BN7 1XU

Distributed in Australia by Capricorn Link (Australia) Pty Ltd.,
P.O. Box 704, Windsor, NSW 2756 Australia

If you have questions or comments about this book, please contact:
Lark Crafts
67 Broadway
Asheville, NC 28801
828-253-0467

Manufactured in China

ISBN 13: 978-1-60059-624-7

For information about custom editions, special sales, premium and corporate purchases, please
contact Sterling Special Sales Department at 800-805-5489 or specialsales@sterlingpub.com.

One dollar from the sale of each specifically marked copy of this book sold through normal
channels of book trade distribution will be donated to Global Impact (www.charity.org),
an organization which promotes humanitarian relief and development.

Contents

Welcome to Craft Hope

As a mother, I spend most days finger painting, playing hide and go seek, cleaning the house, and changing diapers. Tiny footsteps (along with cries and laughter) are the background music to my days. Sticky fingerprints leave their impressions on just about every surface.

I started blogging as a way to connect with the outside world, to find women with similar interests, and I soon discovered a crafting community that amazed me. It was made up of women who stayed up late to sew clothes for their children, knit in the carpool line, and spent much of their free time (and we all know how little that is) crafting for others. Our lives became entwined, one blog linking to another, and then another. This community of women scattered across the globe encouraged each other and joined in the handmade movement together.

For two years I blogged, read blogs, and crafted. It was fun to edit out the messier moments of my life and create a site that highlighted the beauty I learned to find in each day simply by focusing on what was close at hand. Then I found myself wanting to do more. In my pre-mama life I was a teacher and fortunate to have traveled the world with my students, so I knew I wanted to instill in my own children the desire to help others and make a difference in the world. That is how Craft Hope was born.

It started with the simple urge to combine my love of crafting with my desire to spread hope to those who have lost hope or feel forgotten and unloved. I made the site and started with a call for handmade pillowcase dresses (I posted a basic pattern) for a children's shelter in Mexico. Twenty-seven dresses arrived in the mail within a few weeks. I moved on to cloth dolls for an orphanage in Nicaragua and quickly got

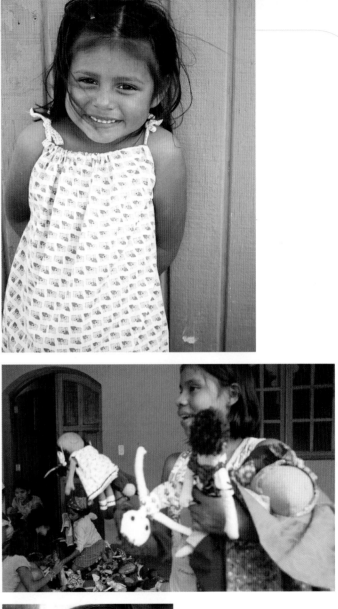

Craft Hope started with a call for pillowcase dresses for a children's shelter in Mexico. Next was soft cloth dolls for an orphanage in Nicaragua. To my surprise, 405 lovingly hand-stitched dolls arrived from crafters around the world.

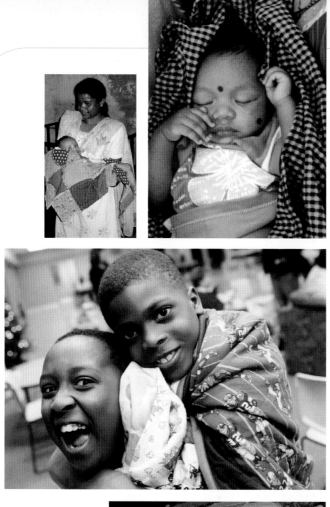

I asked for blankets and other baby items for orphanages in India, and received almost 3,000 donations of handmade goods. Next came sock monkeys of every color and stripe. We ended the first year of Craft Hope by collecting more than 400 handmade quilts. Each homeless child in Grand Rapids, Michigan, received a quilt before Christmas.

a lesson in the power of the Internet: crafters from all over the world began sending in their handcrafted dolls. In what seemed like no time, people from as far away as Brazil, Morocco, Australia, and Japan had sent in 405 handmade dolls. We kept going, gathering burp cloths and crib sheets for orphanages in India, sock monkeys for a children's burn camp in California, and more than enough quilts for each homeless child in Grand Rapids, Michigan.

The growth of the Craft Hope community in a short time was astounding, but it was each individual making up the group that was so inspiring: an 86-year-old woman knitting caps for preemies, a fashion student wanting to do something useful with her remnants, and many, many children learning how to sew dolls and sock monkeys as they also learned that giving really can feel even better than receiving.

In true Craft Hope spirit, within days of deciding to write this book, I had dozens of designers (most of them friends from the craft blog world) returning my emails and enthusiastically agreeing to donate their project designs. You'll find instructions for 32 beautiful craft projects in these pages, each linked with a charity that needs the item. I've provided the web address for each charity so you can find out more about it and contact the organization if you'd like to send the needed item. I've also listed alternative causes and ideas for finding local nonprofits that might need these goods (see Crafting Hope with Care on page 10 for more on making and donating items). Many of the projects involve sewing, but you'll find lots of other crafts, such as soap-making, knitting, stamping, and even macramé.

With my own children, I've now sorted and counted thousands of handcrafted dresses, dolls, sock monkeys, and quilts coming in, and then sent them back out to charities all over the world. Each box that arrives contains its own story of love and hope. I pull out the globe and show my kids where the items are going. We talk about people who are going through a hard time and can use some help and love, and we talk about how some children have no parents or home. Each time, my oldest asks me the same question about the suffering of others: Why? And each time the question breaks my heart. I don't have an answer, except to Craft Hope.

Crafting Hope with Care

Ask anyone who's already crafting for a cause, and they'll tell you that they get back much more than they give. The truth is, giving just plain feels good. But it's also true that giving can be complicated. To give in a way that is respectful, responsible, and empowers the recipient takes a certain amount of care. Here are a few things to keep in mind before plunging into the joy of crafting for others.

Many crafters took care to make dolls with brown hair and eyes for the orphans in Nicaragua. The dolls are used in the therapy the children receive to help them recover from the experiences that brought them to the orphanage.

Giving Thoughtfully

Whenever you craft items for a person or an organization, you'll want to be sure that what you make is both appropriate and useful. Every charity selected for this book, while extremely appreciative of the anticipated donations, also expressed concern that they might receive inappropriate or unneeded goods. Nonprofits almost always operate on a shoestring, and trying to dispose of unneeded or inappropriate donations costs precious time and money. That's one reason I provided website information instead of an address for most causes. Always contact the organization a project is linked with before sending any items to make sure those particular goods can still be used. Books are in print a long time, and needs change. Never send unsolicited items to a charity. I've provided alternative places to donate (including ideas for giving locally) for each project to make finding the perfect match easier.

We knew our quilts would be going to children of all different ages, so we asked for a range of patterns and fabrics.

Of course, you'd want any homemade items you give to a stranger to be every bit as well made and beautiful as something you'd like for yourself or would give to a loved one or friend. But you'll also need to think about the situation of the adult or child receiving the items. Try to imagine the recipient's life. What is the weather most of the time? Does the person have access to a washing machine? Might the recipient have certain religious beliefs or cultural ideas that will affect your choice of color or the decoration on your items? A wool dress is going to be of little use in The Dominican Republic, and a quilt featuring Christian symbolism would be an inappropriate gift for a Muslim child. Learning a bit about the culture or religion of the people you are trying to help is a loving, respectful act. It's also a wonderful opportunity to teach your own children if they are helping you with your Craft Hope projects.

Also, while many organizations do need material goods, please remember that money is the lifeblood of most nonprofits. It doesn't feel as special to send money, but that's what pays for transportation, food, medical supplies, and workers' salaries. Consider including a financial donation, even a small amount, to the charities you're sending handmade goods to. Again, this can be a meaningful way to get your children involved. Encouraging them to put aside a bit of their allowance each week or to sell lemonade to raise money for a cause they care about will go a long way toward nurturing the kind of compassion that we all want to see in our children.

I was so pleased when I learned Lark Crafts wanted to donate one dollar from the sale of each Craft Hope book to Global Impact (www.charity.org), an umbrella organization for more than 50 international charities. Then, tragically, just as this book was about to go to print, the earthquake hit Haiti. We knew this was definitely a situation where money was needed much more than handmade goods. With the help of many members of the Craft Hope community, we quickly set up a Craft Hope for Haiti shop on www.etsy.com, with 100 percent of the money from sales going to Doctors without Borders. We were completely overwhelmed by the response—both from crafters generously donating items to sell and from buyers. We raised more than $27,000 in 10 days. (Please see Konbit Sante on page 35 and Giving Children Hope on page 69 for information on other nonprofits working in Haiti.)

Giving Locally

By getting involved in your community and finding out where the needs are close to home, you'll be able to make an impact in your own backyard. In your town, there are likely children's homes, homeless shelters, nursing homes, hospitals, and many other organizations that need you. Your neighbor, coworker, or a family member might be in need of the comfort of something handmade right now.

Once you start donating your handmade items locally, you may also be inspired to donate your time as well and really get to know the people you are helping. Make it a family day and bring the whole gang to work at the local soup kitchen, to read books to the children at a storytime, or volunteer to process clothing or food donations. The list goes on and on. Chances are you'll discover that the very people you'd like to help have an awful lot to give and teach you.

A Konbit Sante doctor in Haiti talks to a traditional birth attendant. The newborn's simple cap, made from a T-shirt, helps to retain precious body heat. Instructions for the hats, designed by Amanda Soule, and information about Konbit Sante, can be found on page 35.

Our Craft Hope for Haiti shop on www.etsy.com raised more than $27,000 for Doctors without Borders in 10 days.

Giving and Empowering

"Give a man a fish, you have fed him for today. Teach a man to fish, you have fed him for a lifetime." Making handmade items with love and attention and then giving them to someone who is materially less fortunate than you is an act of kindness. And this world can certainly use kindness. But it's important not to think of those we might want to help as helpless. And while meeting someone's immediate needs is important, empowering someone to take care of his or her own needs is equally important. As you become aware of all the various people in difficult situations, both around the world and down the street, educate yourself about the different political, cultural, and socio-economic forces that might be contributing to the situation. What's the larger picture, and what are the steps you, as one individual, could take to start to make a difference?

Zach Bonner started his The Little Red Wagon Foundation (page 57) when he was eight. In 2010, Zach (now 13) will walk from Tampa, Florida, to Los Angeles, California, to raise awareness of the more than 1.3 million homeless children living in the United States.

It may be that you want to get involved in a cause through political or other action, or you may want to dig right in and start to help people empower themselves. A book tote is a thoughtful gift to give someone who is learning to read. But if you also became that person's literacy tutor, you could make an incredible difference in his or her life. You can donate scarves to a local women's shelter, but you might also want to donate yarn and needles and perhaps knitting lessons to teach the women there a valuable and enriching skill.

A woman at the Mioyo Pamoja sewing co-op in Tanzania. These women want to grow their business and intend to empower themselves and others in their villages.

A program that exemplifies this idea is Hearts in Unity. With the mission of helping women to help themselves, the Wisconsin-based nonprofit started two sewing co-ops in Tanzania in 2008. The Mioyo Pamoja ("Hearts in Unity" in Swahili) sewing and knitting co-ops are located in the villages of Mweka (on the slopes of Mt. Kilimanjaro) and in Seela (on the slopes of Mt. Meru). The goal of these co-ops is to provide long-term, sustainable employment opportunities for the local women, and for the youth that they will train to become tailors and knitters. The women are sewing school uniforms and other clothing items for local villagers and have recently purchased a knitting machine. Empowered with the tools and skills to earn income, these women have the opportunity to overcome the poverty of their daily lives and to make a difference in the lives of others. The co-op members have asked for donations of fabric, yarn, and other sewing/knitting supplies such as thread, buttons, and zippers for the school uniforms and clothing they make. You can find out more about donating to the Mioyo Pamoja co-ops (and hand-crafted items needed in Tanzania) at www.heartsinunity. org. Designers Amy Butler and Heather Bailey have both generously donated fabric from their collections for Craft Hope to send to the Mioyo Pamoja co-ops. Check in your own community and you may find (or want to start!) a similar program.

The more you become involved with and really learn about people whose circumstances differ from your own, the more likely you are to see them as real people with a lot to give. Humbly lending a hand while acknowledging the value of us all can be life changing for all parties. I hope that becoming a part of Craft Hope is just such an experience for you.

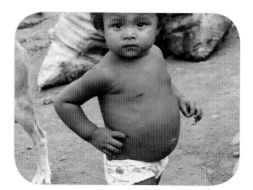

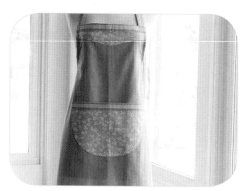

The Projects & Charities

Designer: *Jade Sims*

Pillowcase Dress

Put your pillowcase stash to good use with this quick-sew pattern. The first project on the Craft Hope website, these dresses delighted the young girls in Mexico who received them.

Basic Sewing Kit (page 124)

Standard pillowcase

Water-soluble fabric marker

Thread to match the pillowcase

12 inches (30.5 cm) of elastic, ½ inch (1.3 cm) wide

60 inches (152.4 cm) of bias tape

Lace or ribbon trim (optional)

1. Since you can't measure the child who will be receiving the dress, use the following guidelines to determine the correct length for the body of the dress: six to 12 months, 15 inches (38.1 cm); 2 toddler, 19 inches (48.3 cm); 3 toddler, 21 inches (53.3 cm). For larger sizes, simply add 2 inches (5 cm) in length for each additional year of age.

2. Measure up from the open end of the pillowcase, and mark the chosen length with the water-soluble fabric marker.

3. Cut straight across the width of the pillowcase, through both layers, at the marked length. This cut edge will become the top of the dress.

4. To make the armholes, start at the top of the cut edge, and draw a J-shape down each side of the pillowcase (figure 1). Make each J 2 inches (5 cm) wide and 3 inches (7.6 cm) long for a small child, and 3 inches (7.6 cm) wide and 4 inches (10.2 cm) long for a large child. Cut out the armholes.

5. Sew casings for the elastic on the front and back of the dress. On the front of the dress, turn the cut edge under ¼ inch (6 mm), and press. Turn under again ¾ inch (1.9 cm), and press. Sew along this folded edge. Repeat on the back of the dress.

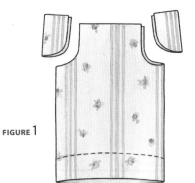

FIGURE 1

Charity

Pan de Vida
www.pdvmex.org

The Pan de Vida children's shelter is a home for abandoned, disadvantaged, and orphaned children in Sandoval, Mexico. The organization provides housing, food, security, and an education for the children. The Pan de Vida shelter was the first organization to which Craft Hope donated handmade items. The pillowcase dresses for the children were lovingly received and appreciated. Other items for the shelter included bandana shorts, blankets, backpacks, and dolls.

OTHER APPROPRIATE CHARITIES FOR THE PILLOWCASE DRESS:

Miracle Foundation (page 73)

Youth Action International (page 49)

Orphanages

6. Cut the elastic in half, making two 6-inch (15.2 cm) pieces. Attach a safety pin to one end of one elastic piece, and pull it through the front casing. Make sure the other end doesn't slip into the casing. Gather the fabric to the length of elastic. Stitch across each end of the casing to hold the elastic in place. Repeat this step on the back, using the second piece of elastic.

7. Complete the dress by binding the armholes with the bias tape. Cut the length of bias tape in half, making two 30-inch (76.2 cm) pieces. Mark the midpoint of each length at 15 inches (38.1 cm). Pin one piece of bias tape over the edge of an armhole with the center fold of the tape covering the raw edge. Match the midpoint mark with the side seams.

8. Using a zigzag stitch, sew the bias tape to the armhole. To prevent unraveling, sew the entire length of the bias tape to close the open edge. Repeat steps 7 and 8 for the other armhole, using the remaining length of bias tape.

9. (Optional) Embellish the dress with lace trim or ribbon by sewing it around the dress on the hemline of the pillowcase.

I Spy Quilt

Quilts are comforting and colorful, and this one is playful as well. Novelty fabrics provide the images for a game of I Spy—a great way to bring a little warmth to a child without the comfort of a home.

Designer: **Kathy Mack**

I Spy Quilt

Hope Note

Craft Hope has started a meaningful dialogue between my daughter and me about how it is our responsibility as humans to help whenever and wherever we can. She keeps asking me what else the kids need and if we can send it to Craft Hope. This is the kind of person I had hoped to help her become.

Mary Ellen, New Jersey

Basic Sewing Kit (page 124)

⅛ yard (11.4 cm) each of 25 assorted novelty print cottons

¼ yard (22.9 cm) each of 10 assorted cotton solids

½ yard (45.7 cm) of a light-color solid cotton

¾ yard (68.6 cm) of print cotton for the wide border

1⅜ yard (1.2 m) of print cotton for the backing

½ yard (45.7 cm) of print cotton for the binding

All-purpose cotton-wrapped thread for piecing

Rotary cutter and mat

Ruler

Low-loft cotton batting

Walking foot for machine quilting

Machine quilting thread, 40-weight in variegated cotton

Note: All fabric is 44 inches (111.8 cm) wide

Seam Allowance
¼ inch (6 mm), unless otherwise noted

What You Cut

Novelty Prints
25 rectangles, one from each print, each 5 x 3 inches (12.7 x 7.6 cm)

Assorted Solids
25 rectangles, each 5 x 3 inches (12.7 x 7.6 cm)
10 strips, one of each color, cut across the width of the fabric. Vary the width of the strips between 1, 2, and 3 inches (2.5, 5, and 7.6 cm).

Light-color Solid Cotton
8 strips, each 1½ x 44 inches (3.8 x 111.8 cm), cut across the width of the fabric

Print Cotton for the Wide Border
4 strips, each 5 x 44 inches (12.7 x111.8 cm), cut across the width of the fabric

Print Cotton for the Binding
5 strips, each ½ x 44 inches (1.3 x 111.8 cm), cut across the width of the fabric

---

1. Pair each rectangle of the novelty prints with a complementary rectangle cut from the assorted solids. Starting at the upper left corner with a novelty print, arrange the pairs on your work surface or design wall into a pleasing pattern. Alternate the prints with solids to form a grid that is five blocks across and ten down. Note: Step back or take a digital picture to analyze the final layout for color and balance before sewing the rectangles together.

2. Piece the top using the all-purpose thread. First, pin and sew each of the five vertical columns, pressing the seam allowances down. Then, join the columns together, pressing the seam allowances to one side.

3. With right sides together, pin a light-color solid strip to one side of the pieced top. Position the strip with the selvage ends extending beyond the top and bottom edges. Trim the excess to make the edges flush. Sew the strip to the pieced top. Press the seam allowance toward the center. Repeat for the other side. Then repeat to sew strips to the top and bottom edges of the pieced top.

4. Cut each strip of the assorted solids in half to measure 22 inches (55.9 cm) in length. Arrange the solid strips on your work surface, varying the widths to create visual interest. With right sides facing, pin the strips together along their long edges, and sew. Press the seam allowances open. Add strips until the piece measures at least 15 inches (38.1 cm) wide.

Charity

Project Night Night
www.projectnightnight.org

Project Night Night donates more than 25,000 canvas tote bags each year to homeless children. Each bag includes a blanket, an age-appropriate book, and a stuffed animal. The project's objective is to deliver a night night package to every homeless child in the United States who needs one to feel secure, cozy, ready to learn, and significant. Blankets are the most difficult items for the organization to obtain, and they especially appreciate homemade ones.

OTHER APPROPRIATE CHARITIES FOR THE QUILT:

Margaret's Hope Chest (page 45)

Little Red Wagon Foundation (page 57)

Any child undergoing medical treatment or convalescing

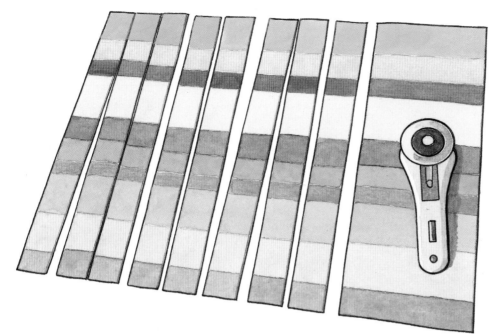

FIGURE 1

5. Using the rotary cutter, mat, and ruler, cut eight 2-inch (5 cm) strips across the width of the pieced fabric (figure 1). Divide the strips into pairs. Sew the short ends together to create four strips for the pieced border.

6. As you did in step 3, pin and sew the pieced borders to the edges of the quilt top, pressing the seam allowances open as you go.

7. As you did in step 3, pin and sew another light-color solid border to the edges of the quilt top, pressing the seam allowances open as you go.

8. As you did in step 3, pin and sew the wide print border to the edges of the quilt top, pressing the seam allowances open as you go.

9. Lay the cotton print for the backing right side down on your work surface. Lay the cotton batting on top of it. Then lay the pieced top, right side up, onto both layers. Baste the layers together. Trim the backing and batting to leave a 1-inch (2.5 cm) border around the edges of the pieced top.

10. Use a walking foot on your sewing machine to machine quilt the pieced top. On the first column, count down five rectangles to the piecing line. Starting at the outermost edge (just inside the border), sew from side to side, crossing the piecing line back and forth with a wavy line. At the end of the row, turn, and stitch in the ditch to the next row. Repeat until all horizontal rows have been quilted with wavy lines. Quilt the vertical rows using the same wavy-line technique.

11. When you've finished quilting horizontally and vertically, stitch in the ditch around all edges of the pieced center.

12. Stitch a wavy line on each of the light solid borders to create a picture-frame effect. On the pieced border, topstitch ¼ inch (6 mm) in from each edge all the way around. On the outer border, stitch back and forth from the outer and inner edges to quilt a large zigzag pattern.

13. Bind the edges. Trim the batting and backing flush to the edges of the pieced top. Lay the short end of one binding strip on another at a 90° angle with right sides facing. Then sew them together on a 45° angle. Continue in this way until you have one long strip. Trim the angles, being careful to avoid cutting the stitches. Press the seams open. Fold the binding strip in half, wrong sides together and long edges aligned, pressing the fold as you go.

14. Pin the binding to the quilt with right sides facing and raw edges aligned. Sew the binding to the quilt, mitering the corners as you go (see Binding Edges with Mitered Corners on page 39). Turn the binding over the raw edges and hand stitch to the quilt, turning the raw edge of the binding under as you sew.

Designer: *Kaari Meng*

Apron

Appealing yet practical, this apron will work well in the kitchen or the garden. To make aprons appropriate for both men and women, use neutral colors and fabrics.

Basic Sewing Kit (page 124)	Transfer paper
Template (page 133)	Thread in a coordinating color
1 yard (.9 m) of brown linen	**Seam Allowance**
¼ yard (22.9 cm) of floral print cotton	½ inch (1.3 cm), unless otherwise noted
¼ yard (22.9 cm) of striped cotton	

1. Copy and enlarge the template pieces on page 133. Cut the apron from the linen, the yoke and pocket from the floral print cotton, and the yoke and pocket trim from the striped cotton.

2. Cut a strip from the striped cotton, 3¼ x 23 inches (8.3 x 58.4 cm), for the neck straps. Then cut two strips from the striped cotton, each 1¾ x 40 inches (4.4 x 101.6 cm), for the ties.

3. On the right side of the apron, use the transfer paper to mark the placement for the yoke and pocket.

4. Press the lower edge of the yoke (with the point) under ½ inch (1.3 cm). Pin the yoke on the apron with the wrong side of the yoke facing the right side of the apron and aligning the raw edges. Topstitch the yoke to the apron, ¼ inch (6 mm) in from all edges.

5. Press one long edge of the yoke trim under ½ inch (1.3 cm). With the right side of the trim facing the wrong side of the apron, align the raw edge of the trim to the top of the apron. Pin and sew. Trim the seam allowance to ¼ inch (6 mm). Turn the trim to the right side of the apron, and press. Topstitch the yoke trim ¼ inch (6 mm) in from both long edges.

Charity

The Food Project
www.thefoodproject.org

The Food Project's mission is to grow a thoughtful and productive community of youth and adults from diverse backgrounds who work together to build a sustainable food system. It produces healthy food for residents of Boston and its suburbs while providing leadership opportunities for youth. Most important, it strives to inspire and support others to create change in their own communities. The Food Project works with teens and thousands of volunteers on its farms to grow nearly a quarter-million pounds of food annually without chemical pesticides and donates thousands of pounds of this food to local shelters.

OTHER APPROPRIATE CHARITIES FOR THE APRON:

Youth Action International (page 49)

A nonprofit bakery

A local food bank or soup kitchen

6. Press one long edge of the pocket trim under ½ inch (1.3 cm). With the right side of the trim facing the wrong side of the pocket, align the raw edge of the trim with the top edge of the pocket. Pin and sew. Trim the seam allowance to ¼ inch (6 mm). Turn the trim to the right side of the pocket, and press. Topstitch the pocket trim ¼ inch (6 mm) in from both long edges.

7. Notch the seam allowance on the curved edge of the pocket. Press the raw edge under ½ inch (1.3 cm). Pin the pocket on the apron using the placement marks as your guide. Attach the pocket by edge stitching close to the pressed edge, leaving the top edge open. Topstitch ¼ inch (6 mm) in from the edge stitching.

8. Clip the seam allowances along the curved edges of the armholes. Press the edges, including the yoke and trim, under ¼ inch (6 mm). Turn under again ½ inch (1.3 cm), press, and edge stich.

9. Press both long edges of the neck strap in ½ inch (1.3 cm). Fold the strap in half lengthwise with wrong sides facing and the pressed edges aligned. Topstitch ¼ inch (6 mm) in from both long edges. Press both short ends under ½ inch (1.3 cm).

10. On the wrong side of the apron, pin the pressed ends of the strap to the top of the apron. Topstitch the straps in place, as shown in figure 1.

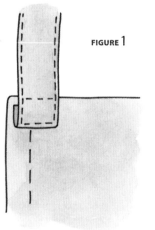

FIGURE 1

11. Hem the apron. Turn the bottom edge under ¼ inch (6 mm), and press. Turn under again ½ inch (1.3 cm), press, and then edge stitch close to the pressed edge.

12. Make the ties. Press the long edges of the ties in ¼ inch (6 mm). Fold each strap in half lengthwise with wrong sides facing and the pressed edges aligned. Topstitch ¼ inch (6 mm) in from both long edges. Fold one raw end of each strap under ¼ inch (6 mm). Turn under again ½ inch (1.3 cm), and then topstitch close to the pressed edges.

13. Press the sides of the apron under ¼ inch (6 mm). Turn under again ½ inch (1.3 cm), and press. On the wrong side of the apron, slip the raw end of one tie under the pressed edge of the apron (figure 2). Then topstitch the side of the apron along the pressed edge, sewing the tie in as you go. Flip the tie over the stitching, then topstitch the outer edge of the side seam, stitching though the tie to secure it as you go (figure 3). Repeat on the other side.

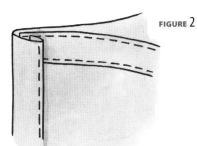

FIGURE 2

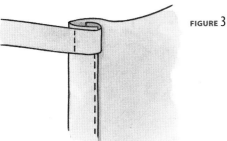

FIGURE 3

Designer: *Vickie Howell*

Star Stitch Knit Scarf

Scarves are easy to make and provide yards of warmth for anyone who lives in a cold climate. Designed for a charity that sends red scarves to young people from foster care who are starting college, this project is a great way to give while you knit.

Approx 208yd/190m of red (5) bulky weight yarn

6.5 mm (size 10½ U.S.) knitting needles

Tapestry Needle

Gauge
4.5 sts per inch (2.5 cm) in k1, p1 ribbed pattern

NOTE: The scarf is made with a special star stitch. To Make Star (MS) you purl 3 sts together, leaving the sts on the left-hand needle. Wrap the yarn around the needle, then purl the same 3 sts together again. See page 126 for knitting abbreviations and yarn weight chart.

1. CO 21 sts.

Rows 1-14: Work in k1, p1 rib to end.
Row 15 (RS): P1, *k1, p1; rep from * to end.
Row 16: K1, *MS, k1; rep from * to end.
Row 17: Repeat row 15.
Row 18: K1, p1, k1, *MS, k1; rep from * to last 2 sts, p1, k1.
Rows 19–284: Repeat rows 15–18.
Row 285–298: Work in k1, p1 rib to end. BO.

2. Finish by weaving in the ends. Block if necessary.

The scarf was knit using 2 balls of Malabrigo Chunky (100% kettle-dyed pure Merino wool, 3.5oz/99g = 104yd/95m per ball), in color: Sealing Wax 102.

Hope Note

I have received my care package, and I really can't describe how I felt when I was wearing that red scarf. It made me smile throughout the whole day because, although no one knew it was hand-made for me or that it was a gift, I knew it was and that made it special. Thank you SO MUCH.

Sheryl, Florida

Charity

Orphan Foundation of America
www.orphan.org

Each year 25,000 teens "age out" of the foster care system in the United States. The Orphan Foundation of America works to support their post-secondary education goals and mobilize the community at large to assist them. It awards $15 million annually in funding to foster youth who attend college and specialized training programs. The organization also provides mentoring, internships, care packages, and family-like support. Their Red Scarf Project collects red knit or crocheted scarves to add to Valentine's Day care packages sent to OFA students enrolled in college or trade school. Because it has limited means for storage, OFA asks that you send scarves only during specific time periods, which you can find on its website.

OTHER APPROPRIATE CHARITIES FOR THE SCARF:

SOME (page 41)
LOWO Child & Family Services (page 77)
Local homeless shelters

Designer: *Jhoanna Monte*

Soft Cloth Doll

The simple gift of a doll can provide a child with an instant best friend. This project—the second on the Craft Hope website—yielded more than 400 dolls from crafters in a variety of countries, including Mexico, Norway, and Australia. When designing your doll, keep in mind the skin, hair, and eye color of the child who might receive it.

Basic Sewing Kit (page 124)	Polyester fiberfill
Template (page 132)	Embroidery floss
Fabric scraps, none smaller than 5 x 7 inches (12.7 x 17.8 cm)	Buttons (optional)
	Trim (optional)
Felt	**Seam Allowance**
Transfer paper	¼ inch (6 mm), unless otherwise noted

1. Trace each of the labeled templates on page 132, and cut them out. Be sure to trace the marks for the arm guides on each piece B and the marks for the opening on piece C.

> **TIP** Use your colorful fabric scraps to craft this huggable cutie. Mix, match, and coordinate the fabrics at will. Add buttons, bows, and trim, but attach securely, and don't add embellishments if meant for children under age three.

2. Trace or pin the pattern pieces to your chosen fabric scraps, and cut out the specified number for each piece. Cut pieces F and G from the felt. Note that pieces A, B, C, D, and E already include a ¼-inch (6 mm) seam allowance. Transfer the marks for the arm guides and opening onto the fabric using the transfer paper.

Charity

ORPHANetwork
www.orphanetwork.org

The ORPHANetwork provides a safe and loving home for children in Nicaragua. It runs Casa Bernabe, an orphanage complex in Vera Cruz, near the capital city of Managua. The home serves orphaned, abandoned, and neglected children ranging from three years old to late teens. The faith-based nonprofit believes in empowering local leadership to solve local problems. The dolls are used at the orphanage for counseling; they provide each girl with something that is hers alone.

OTHER APPROPRIATE CHARITIES FOR THE DOLL:

Giving Children Hope (page 69)
Local programs for foster children
Holiday toy drives

A friend and I used to have craft nights back in Boston. Recently, to keep in touch, we signed up to make dolls for the orphanage in Nicaragua, and we chat via Skype as we sew (sewing is much more fun with company!).

Amy, Japan

3. Make the arms and legs. With right sides facing, sew two arm pieces (D) together. Leave the diagonal edge open for turning and stuffing. Repeat to make the other arm. Turn them right side out, and stuff each arm using the polyester fiberfill. Once stuffed, stitch the openings closed. Do the same for the legs, leaving the top of the leg open for turning and stuffing.

4. Sew the head and body. With right sides facing, sew one piece A to one piece B. With right sides facing, sew one piece C to piece B. Repeat for the other side of the doll. Press all seams open.

5. Center the face (F) on the head on one side of the doll. Use the embroidery floss and a hand stitch of your choice to attach the face by sewing around the edge. In the same way, position the cheeks on the face, and stitch. Embroider the eyes and mouth. If you wish, you can cut a small piece of felt for parted hair or bangs, and stitch to attach. Note: You could attach and embroider the face after stuffing the doll; however, it's much easier to do when the piece is flat.

6. If you're embellishing the doll, add buttons, trim, embroidery—whatever you like!—securely to the front of the doll.

7. Assemble the doll. Lay one side of the doll right side up. Following figure 1, position the arms on piece B between the marked arm guides. Arms should be pointing in and down. Pin the arms in place. Position the legs with the toes pointing in whatever direction you choose, out or in, and pin.

8. Lay the other side of the doll, with right sides facing, on top of the piece with the pinned arms and legs. Align all edges, and pin them together. Stitch the doll, leaving the opening you marked on piece C unsewn.

9. Clip the curve of the neck, making sure to avoid cutting into the stitching. Notch the curve around the head and around the curved corners at the bottom of the dress. Turn the doll, and stuff. Blind-stitch the opening closed.

FIGURE 1

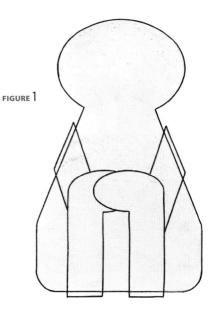

Instructions for Eren's doll design can be found at: http://www.larkbooks.com/crafts/bonus.

SPREADING HOPE IN NICARAGUA

Eren Hays San Pedro headed up Craft Hope's second project for a charity close to her heart. On a return visit to the Casa Bernabe orphange near Managua, Nicaragua, she learned they needed dolls to help counsel the children. Craft Hope seemed like the perfect answer. After collecting over 400 dolls from Craft Hope participants around the world, Eren arrived in Nicaragua with suitcases packed with beautiful dolls.

The caregivers at Casa Bernabe were overwhelmed to learn that mothers, grandmothers, children, and crafting groups around the world were thinking of their children. One woman said that when she put the children to bed that evening, she'd tell them they were each so special that someone across the globe was thinking about them while making the dolls they were now holding.

A few days later, Eren returned to the dorm but couldn't find the dolls. When she asked a caregiver where they were, the woman lifted a pillow to show a doll hidden under it. She said the children put their most prized possesions under their pillows for safekeeping. Sure enough, each pillow had a doll beneath it, just waiting to be loved that evening.

Designer: *Amanda Soule*

Simple-Knot Newborn Cap

Tiny newborns—especially preemies—need to retain body heat to survive. Made from repurposed cotton T-shirts, these sweet caps will help the wee ones stay warm. Create several, as they're needed by a multitude of charitable organizations.

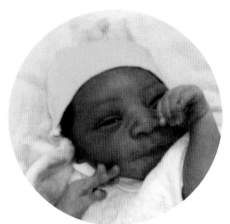

Basic Sewing Kit (page 124)

Template (page 132)

One knit cotton T-shirt (an adult size makes two)

All-purpose thread, coordinating color

Seam Allowance
⅝ inch (1.6 cm), unless otherwise noted

1. Copy and enlarge the template on page 132.

2. Turn the T-shirt wrong side out with right sides facing.

3. Lay the shirt flat on your cutting surface. Place the template on top of the shirt, aligning the bottom edge of the template with the bottom hem of the shirt. Cut two pieces at the same time by cutting through both layers of fabric.

4. Pin the two hat pieces together, keeping the right sides facing.

5. Adjust your sewing machine or serger as needed for sewing knits. If you're using a sewing machine, set the stitch for a tight zigzag.

> **TIP** Sergers are great for sewing jersey knits, but if you don't own one you can get the same results by using a sewing machine and following a few tips. First, read your manual for specific details on adjusting the tension and the pressure foot when working with knits. Use a ballpoint needle; the rounded tip glides between the fibers, which prevents damage to the fabric and helps you avoid skipped stitches. Be sure to run a test on a fabric scrap. Finally, don't pull the fabric through. Let it glide under the presser foot to avoid puckering.

6. Starting at one edge of the hem, stitch up one side of the hat and down the other, backstitching at each end. If you used a sewing machine, trim the entire seam, being careful to avoid cutting the stitches, and use a zigzag stitch to overcast the seam allowance.

7. Turn the hat right side out. If needed, use a knitting needle to gently push out the tip. Make a simple overhand knot approximately 3 inches (7.6 cm) down from the top point.

Charity

Konbit Sante Cap-Haitien Health Partnership
www.konbitsante.org

Even before the devastating earthquake in January, 2010, Haiti was the poorest country in the Western Hemisphere. Two-thirds of all Haitians were malnourished and one out of every 12 Haitian children did not survive to age five. Konbit Sante Cap-Haitien Health Partnership is a Maine-based volunteer partnership to save lives and improve health care in northern Haiti. Konbit Sante works with the Haitian Ministry of Health and with Haitian colleagues to develop programs to improve care in pediatrics, internal medicine, infection control, neighborhood outreach, and women's health. It works to enhance education in all areas of medicine and mental health, to make improvements at local hospitals, and to deliver containers of mostly badly needed medical equipment and supplies. Amanda Soule collected 5,523 of these caps to send to Konbit Sante through her Mama to Mama site.

OTHER APPROPRIATE CHARITIES FOR THE NEWBORN CAPS:

Giving Children Hope (page 69)

Care Bags Foundation (page 53)

Pediatric units at local hospitals

Designer: *Manda McGrory*

Patchwork Pillow

Brighten someone's day with this cheerful piece of patchwork. Whether welcoming someone to a new home or just providing support, this colorful cushion will bring comfort in any setting.

Basic Sewing Kit (page 124)

¼ yard (22.9 cm) each of 10 different red cotton prints

¼ yard (22.9 cm) each of two different gray cotton prints

Muslin, one 19-inch (48.3 cm) square

Quilt batting, one 19-inch (48.3 cm) square

¼ yard (22.9 cm) of a natural-color linen

1 yard (.9 m) of red bias binding

¼ yard (22.9 cm) of fabric for the binding

17 x 17 inch (43.2 x 43.2 cm) pillow form

Seam Allowance
¼ inch (6 mm), unless otherwise noted

1. Cut each of the different red and gray print fabrics into strips that are 2 inches (5 cm) wide.

2. Choose any strip to start. Cut it approximately 6 inches (15.2 cm) in length, and lay it right side up on your work surface. Choose a different strip, and cut it a bit longer or shorter than the first piece. Lay it short-end-to-short-end next to the first piece. Continue in this way until you have a row made of three or four different fabrics that is 19 inches (48.3 cm) long. Note: Each row must be a minimum of 19 inches (48.3 cm) long. Since the finished pillow will be approximately 16¼ inches (41.9 cm) square, you'll need this extra width to accommodate the seam allowances.

> **TIP** When laying out your patchwork pieces, try to avoid placing the same prints too close together in the overall design. Don't be afraid to move prints around until you find a pleasing pattern. Try not to analyze too much—it's all about being creative!

3. Continue laying the strips down in this way until you have 12 rows. Vary the length of each piece, and remember to use one of the gray prints among the red every now and then.

4. Sew the pieces together to make the rows. Start with the first two pieces of the top row. Lay them right sides together, and stitch. Press the seams flat. Continue sewing and pressing the other pieces until you have one complete, pieced row. Repeat for the remaining 11 rows.

Charity

Jewish Family Service of Seattle
www.jfsseattle.org

Jewish Family Service of Seattle has been delivering essential human services to alleviate suffering, sustain healthy relationships, and support people in times of need for more than 117 years. The organization embraces the concept of helping others help themselves with an extensive range of programs that serve more than 12,500 people each year in the greater Seattle area. The organization will use the patchwork pillows for programs that help refugees and immigrants settle into houses, assist the homeless moving into new homes, and aid women in domestic violence shelters (who often have little to call their own).

OTHER APPROPRIATE CHARITIES FOR THE PILLOW:

MD Anderson Cancer Center (page 103)

Local housing programs

Local women's shelters

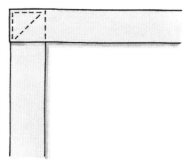

FIGURE 1

5. Sew the rows together, starting with the top two rows. Lay them right sides together, and stitch. Press the seam to one side. Continue sewing and pressing the other rows in this way until the pieced pillow top is complete. Set aside.

6. Lay the muslin square right side down on your work surface, and place the quilt batting over it. Lay the pieced top right side up on top of the muslin and batting. Trim the muslin and batting through both layers to be slightly larger all the way around than the pieced top. Pin through all layers over the entire pieced top.

7. Quilt the top. Starting at the center row and working toward your right, align the edge of your presser foot to the seam line. Stitch through all layers. The stitching will be approximately ¼ inch (6 mm) from the seam. Remove the pins as you stitch. Smooth the fabric, but don't pull it as you sew. Repeat for all rows on this half. Note: Starting at the center and quilting one half at a time helps prevent the fabric from puckering. Turn the fabric, and quilt the second half as you did the first.

8. Trim the threads and square the top to a 16½-inch (41.9 cm) square. Trim the edges to size as needed. Lay the quilted top aside. Note: A 16½ x 16½ inch (41.9 x 41.9 cm) pillowcase will accomodate a 17 x 17 inch (43.2 x 43.2 cm) pillow form. It's a snug fit, but it crates a firm pillow.

9. Make the envelope back. Cut two pieces of the natural-color linen, each 16½ x 12 inches (41.9 x 30.5 cm). Using approximately 18 inches (45.7 cm) of the red bias binding for each edge, bind one long edge on each piece. Note: If you prefer, you can hem the edges instead.

10. Lay the quilted top right side down. Lay one of the hemmed linen pieces, right side up, on top of it. Align the raw edges, and pin. Repeat with the other piece of linen to overlap the first. Sew around the edges through all layers. Do not trim the seam allowance.

11. Make the binding. First cut the fabric for the binding into strips that are ½ inch (1.3 cm) wide. Lay the short end of one binding strip on another at a 90° angle with right sides facing. Then sew them together on a 45° angle (figure 1).

12. Continue in this way until you have one long strip. You'll need approximately 80 inches (203.2 cm) to bind the pillow. Trim the seam allowances, being careful to avoid cutting the stitches. Press the seams open. Fold and press the strip in half lengthwise with wrong sides together and long edges aligned. Fold one of the short ends under ½ inch (1.3 cm), and press. Attach the binding, making mitered corners as you go (see Binding Edges with Mitered Corners at right).

13. When you get close to your starting point, trim the binding to length, allowing 1½ inches (3.8 cm) for an overlap. Fold the end under ½ inch (1.3 cm), and finish sewing the binding, overlapping the starting point.

14. Turn the binding to the other side of the pillow. The mitered corners will easily fold in place. Hand stitch the binding to the back of the pillow using the blind stitch (page 125).

15. Insert the pillow form.

BINDING EDGES WITH MITERED CORNERS

With right sides together and raw edges aligned, begin sewing the binding to the fabric. Stop sewing ¼ inch (6 mm) from the corner. Fold the binding over itself to create a crease (figure 2). Fold the binding down and rotate the fabric 90°. Don't stitch across the corner; instead stitch ¼ inch (6 mm) in from the edge (figure 3). Continue stitching around the edges and mitering the corners until you get back to your starting place, overlapping the ends for a neat finish. Turn the binding over the raw edge (figure 4), and stitch it to the fabric on the other side.

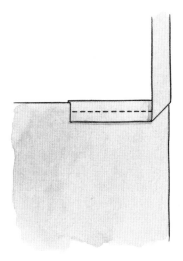

FIGURE 2

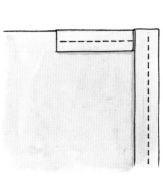

FIGURE 3

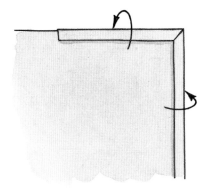

FIGURE 4

Designer: *Jhoanna Monte*

Patchwork Scarf

The gift of a scarf is a little like the gift of a hug—personal, comforting, and warm. This easy patchwork design is a great way to use up your favorite fabric scraps. Keep yours plain and simple, or dress it up with trims, notions, and decorative stitches.

What You Need: Adult Scarf

Basic Sewing Kit (page 124)

1½ yards (1.3 m) of solid linen or cotton

Print fabric scraps for piecing, none smaller than 7 x 3 inches (17.8 x 7.6 cm)

1¾ yards (1.6 m) of solid or print cotton for the lining

7 inches (17.8 cm) of lace trim (optional)

Flannel (optional)

Water-soluble fabric marker (optional)

Large button (optional)

What You Need: Child Scarf

⅛ yard (.1 m) solid linen or cotton

⅛ yard (.1 m) solid or patterned cotton

Print fabric scraps for piecing, none smaller than 3 x 7 inches (7.6 x 17.8 cm)

Flannel (optional)

Seam Allowance
½ inch (1.3 cm), unless otherwise noted

What You Cut: Adult Scarf

Solid Linen or Cotton

1 piece, 7 x 48 inches (17.8 x 122 cm), for piece G

2 pieces, each 7 x 3 inches (17.8 x 7.6 cm), for piece A

Print Fabric Scraps

2 pieces, each 7 x 3 inches (17.8 x 7.6 cm), for piece B

What You Cut: Child Scarf

2¾ x 47 inches (7 x 120 cm) solid linen or cotton

5 x 47 inches (12.7 x 120 cm) solid or patterned cotton

4 pieces, each 2 x 3 inches (5 x 7.6 cm), for pieces C and E

2 pieces, each 3 inches (7.6 cm) square, for piece D

2 pieces, each 7 x 3 inches (17.8 x 7.6 cm), for piece F

Lining

1 piece 7 x 63 inches (17.8 x 160 cm)

8 pieces patterned fabric, each 2¾ x 6 inches (7 x 15.2 cm)

Charity

SOME (So Others Might Eat)
www.some.org

SOME's motto is "Restoring hope and dignity one person at a time." In 1970, Father Horace McKenna and a group of priests, ministers, and laypersons founded So Others Might Eat to help feed the District of Columbia's destitute citizens. Today the interfaith, community-based organization meets the immediate needs of the poor and homeless of the U.S. capital with food, clothing, and health care; it helps break the cycle of homelessness by offering services such as affordable housing, job training, addiction treatment, and counseling to the poor, the elderly, and individuals with mental illness. SOME believes in empowering those who are ready to make real and lasting changes in their lives. It has helped thousands of people get off the streets, transform their lives, and learn to live independently.

OTHER APPROPRIATE CHARITIES FOR THE SCARF:

Safe Place (page 117)

New Orleans Women's Shelter (page 67)

Local women's or homeless shelters

Hope Note

ADULT SCARF

1. Lay out the pieces for the front of the scarf following figure 1.

FIGURE 1

2. Sew the first patchwork panel. Make a strip by sewing one set of pieces C, D, and E together with right sides facing. Press the seams flat. With right sides facing, sew piece F to the top of the patched strip, then sew piece B to the bottom. Sew piece A to piece B. Press all seams flat. Repeat to make the other panel.

3. With right sides together, sew a patchwork panel to each end of piece G. The seams should join pieces F with piece G. Press the seams flat.

4. If you want to add optional lace trim, lay the length of lace across the right side of the fabric on one of the seams joining piece F with piece G. Sew the trim at the seam.

5. Lay the lining on the pieced scarf with right sides together. Align all edges, then pin. Note: If you want a warmer scarf, add a layer of flannel. Cut the flannel the same size as the lining, and then sandwich it between the pieced front and the lining before pinning.

6. Sew around the edges through all layers, leaving a 3-inch (7.6 cm) opening on one end for turning.

7. Trim the corners, being careful to avoid cutting the stitches. Turn the scarf right side out, and push out all of the corners. Press the scarf flat, tucking the raw edges of the opening into the seam allowance.

8. Topstitch around the scarf, using a slightly longer stitch length than you did when sewing the seams.

9. If desired, add a button to secure the scarf when worn. Fold the scarf in half lengthwise with wrong sides facing. Measure 17 inches (43.2 cm) in from one short end, and mark the spot on the fold using a water-soluble fabric marker. Make a horizontal buttonhole at this point. Locate the corresponding point on the other end of the scarf, and sew the button to it.

> **TIP** If you want to use novelty trim to secure the scarf when it is being worn, measure 16.5" (42cm) from one end of the top layer (figure 2). Lay trim across this point and sew trim to the scarf 1 inch (2.5 cm) in from each side, ensuring that the middle portion of the trim is *not* sewn to the scarf.

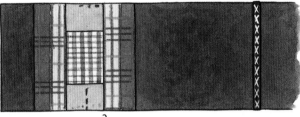

FIGURE 2

CHILD SCARF

1. Sew the eight small patchwork pieces together at their short ends with right sides facing, eventually creating a row of pieces approximately 44½ inches (113 cm) long. Press all seams flat.

2. With right sides facing, join the long edges of the patchwork row with the piece of solid linen or cotton. Press the seam flat. This is now the top layer of the scarf.

3. Lay the cotton lining on the pieced scarf with right sides facing. Align all the edges and pin. Note: If you want a warmer scarf, add a layer of flannel. Cut the flannel to the same size as the lining, and then sandwich it between the pieced front and the lining before pinning.

4. Sew around all four edges of the scarf through all layers, leaving a 3-inch (7.6 cm) opening on one end for turning.

5. Trim the corners, being careful to avoid cutting the stitched seam. Turn the scarf right side out and push out all the corners. Press the scarf flat, tucking the raw edges of the opening into the seam allowance.

6. Topstitch around the scarf ¼ inch (.6 cm) from the edges, using a slightly longer stitch length than you did when sewing the seams. Topstitch the opening closed.

Designer: *Malka Dubrawsky*

Take-Along Quilt

When it was posted on the Craft Hope site as part of a drive to provide quilts for homeless children in Grand Rapids, Michigan, this project drew an international response. Stitchers from as far away as Switzerland, The Netherlands, Uruguay, and Turkey answered the call, creating more than 500 quilts. This colorful comforter is designed to be rolled and carried.

Charity

Margaret's Hope Chest
www.margaretshopechest.com

The mission of Margaret's Hope Chest is to bring hope, comfort, and warmth to people enduring hopeless situations through the gift of a beautifully crafted quilt. In 2005, 80-year-old Margaret Herrema died from a head injury after being shoved to the ground during a purse snatching in a grocery store parking lot. Her daughter and granddaughter founded Margaret's Hope Chest to honor the full and generous life of the woman who had loved quilting for charity. They gave their first quilt to the mother of one of the women convicted of Margaret's death. In the fall of 2009, Craft Hope helped MHC meet its goal of giving a quilt to each homeless child living in the Grand Rapids, Michigan, school district. Quilters from 37 states, four Canadian provinces, and countries as diverse as England, Uruguay, The Netherlands, Switzerland, Turkey, and Scotland sent in more than 500 quilts.

OTHER APPROPRIATE CHARITIES FOR THE QUILT:

Project Night Night (page 21)

Local homeless shelters

Local women's shelters

Basic Sewing Kit (page 124)

9 fat quarters of cotton, each in a different print

¾ yard (68.5 cm) of cotton fabric, 44 inches (111.8 cm) wide, for the strap and binding

Fusible interfacing

4 yards (3.6 m) of cotton flannel for the backing

Thread of coordinating color

Masking tape

Cotton batting

Large safety pins

Water-soluble fabric marker

Button, ¾ inch (1.9 cm)

Seam Allowance
¼ inch (6 mm), unless otherwise noted

What You Cut

Fat Quarters

9 rectangles, one from each print, each 17¼ x 20¾ inches (43.8 x 52.7 cm)

Cotton for Strap and Binding

2 strips, each 3 x 16 inches (7.6 x 40.6 cm), for the strap

6 strips, each 1½ x 44 inches (3.8 x 111.8 cm), cut across the width of the fabric, for the binding

Fusible Interfacing

1 strip, 3 x 16 inches (7.6 x 40.6 cm)

1. Piece the front of the quilt: Pin and then sew two of the rectangles together along one long edge with right sides facing. Press the seam open. Pin and then sew a third rectangle to them to make one strip. Press the seam open. On the right side, topstitch ⅛ inch (3 mm) on either side of the piecing lines. Repeat this step using the remaining rectangles until you have three pieced and topstitched strips.

2. Pin and then sew two of the strips together along one long edge with right sides facing. Press the seam open. Pin and then sew the third strip to them, and press the seam open. On the right side, topstitch ⅛ inch (3 mm) on either side of the piecing lines.

3. Following the manufacturer's instructions, apply the strip of fusible interfacing to the wrong side of one of the pieces cut for the strap. With right sides facing, pin the two pieces for the strap together. Sew along three sides, leaving one of the short ends open for turning. Clip the corners, being careful to avoid cutting the stitches. Turn right side out, using a knitting needle to push out the corners if needed. Press flat.

4. Topstitch ¼ inch (6 mm) in from the sewn edges of the strap. Make a 1-inch (2.5 cm) vertical buttonhole approximately 1½ inches (3.8 cm) from the finished short end of the strap. Set the strap aside.

5. Cut the flannel for the backing into two 2-yard (1.8 m) lengths. Sew them together, right sides facing and selvages aligned, to make one large piece with a center seam. Press the seam open.

6. Working on a large, flat surface, such as a clean floor or large table, place the flannel right side down, smoothing out the fabric from the center. Note: You may find it helpful to use the masking tape to tape the fabric edges to the surface.

7. Lay the cotton batting on top of the flannel, centering it on the center seam. Then lay the pieced top, right side up, on top of both layers, centering it on the batting.

8. Working from the center out, pin through all layers using the safety pins, placing them approximately 4 inches (10.2 cm) apart. Remove the tape at the edges. Trim all layers flush.

9. Fold the quilt in half widthwise with the front sides facing to locate the midpoint of one short edge. Mark the midpoint using the water-soluble fabric marker.

10. On the back of the quilt, center the short, raw end of the strap on the midpoint. Align the raw edges, and pin. The finished edge of the strap with the buttonhole will be facing away from the edge. Baste the strap in place.

11. Make the binding: Lay the short end of one binding strip on another at a 90° angle with right sides facing. Then sew them together at a 45° angle. Continue in this way until you have one long strip. Trim the angles, being careful to avoid cutting the stitches. Press the seams open. Turn one of the short ends of the long strip under ¼ inch (6 mm), and press.

12. Bind the edges. With right sides together and raw edges aligned, and starting at the turned end of the binding, sew the binding to the quilt around all edges, mitering the corners as you go (see Binding Edges with Mitered Corners on page 39). When you get back to the starting point, trim off the excess binding, leaving enough for an overlap. Turn the short end under ¼ inch (6 mm), and finish the stitching to overlap the other end.

13. Fold the binding over the raw edges. Pin the binding to the back of the quilt, turning the raw edge under ¼ inch (6 mm) as you pin. When you get to the strap, turn the seam allowance under on the binding as you have been doing. Once you pass the strap, flip the strap to lie on top of the binding, and pin in place to keep it out of the way when you stitch.

14. Stitch the binding to the back of the quilt by hand or machine. Remove the safety pins holding the layers together.

15. Roll the quilt to place the button. Fold one long edge of the quilt into the center with front sides facing, then fold the other side of the quilt over it. Begin rolling the quilt at the edge without the strap. When the quilt is all rolled up, lay the strap on the roll. Use the fabric marker to mark the placement for the button, and then sew the button at this point.

Hope Note

As someone who was homeless often as a teenager, I can tell you how important something portable is to keep you warm and in touch with normal life. I'm excited to work on this project!

Claire, South Dakota

Designer:
Stefani Austin

Bandana Pants

Lightweight and breathable, these shorts are ideal for children who live in hot climates. Simple and inexpensive to make, they're perfect for a group project.

Basic Sewing Kit (page 124)

Two identical bandanas

Pencil

Matching thread

Pinking shears

Elastic, 1 inch (2.5 cm) wide

Seam Allowance
½ inch (1.3 cm), unless otherwise noted

1. Lay the bandanas one on top of the other with right sides together. Fold them in half, and position them with the long sides facing right.

2. Measure approximately 10 inches (25.4 cm) down from the top along the edge. Use the pencil to mark the point. Measure approximately 2 inches (5 cm) to the left of that point, and mark it with the pencil. Measure up from this point 2 inches (5 cm), and make another mark. Use the pencil to draw a curve connecting the first mark with the third one.

3. Cut the inseam. Start at the first point, and cut through both layers following the curve. When you reach the end of the curve, cut a straight line to the top. Open the folded bandanas, leaving one on top of the other. You should have a big square with mirror-image Js cut out of the top corners.

4. Sew the seam along the cut edges on both sides. For added strength, sew another line of stitching in the seam allowance, ¼ inch (6 mm) away from the first. Use the pinking shears to trim the raw edges.

Charity

Youth Action International
www.youthactioninternational.org

Youth Action International is a network of young international leaders working to rebuild war-torn African communities. With programs in Liberia, Sierra Leone, and Uganda, YAI focuses on three key areas: improving early child development; empowering war-affected youth, former child soldiers, and formerly abducted children; and supporting the needs and development of women and girls at risk of sexual exploitation or domestic violence. More than 100,000 West African youth benefit from YAI's programs. For more information on Youth Action International and its founder, Kimmie Weeks, see page 89.

OTHER APPROPRIATE CHARITIES FOR THE PANTS:

Children of the Forest (page 93)

ORPHANetwork (page 31)

Pan de Vida (page 17)

What a wonderful gift you have given to our family with this group of projects. We have put up a map of the world in our dining room and are putting pins in all of the places Craft Hope is helping people. My little one wants to put a pin in every country. Not a bad life goal, right?

Carrie, Maryland

5. When you hold up the connected bandanas, notice how they resemble a tube where you sewed them. Open the tube and rotate it until the seams are parallel to one another (figure 1). When you lay it back down, it will look like pants, with the curve of the seams as the crotch.

6. Press the seams open, then line up the seams at the crotch and pin. Starting at the bottom inside edge of one pant leg, sew all the way up that leg, through the crotch, and down the inside of the other leg.

7. To make the casing for the elastic, fold the top over 2 inches (5 cm), and press. Starting at one of the seams, sew all the way around, stopping approximately 1 inch (2.5 cm) from where you started sewing.

8. Measure a piece of the elastic to fit a child's waist, plus a little extra for overlapping. This measurement will vary for each child, depending on his age.

9. Hook a safety pin on the end of the elastic, and thread it through the opening until it comes out the other side. Overlap the elastic, and stitch together with a zigzag stitch.

10. Pull the elastic into the casing by putting your hands inside the waist and pushing outward. Sew the opening, being careful to avoid catching the elastic in the stitching. Turn the pants right side out, and you have a pair of perfectly playful pants!

FIGURE 1

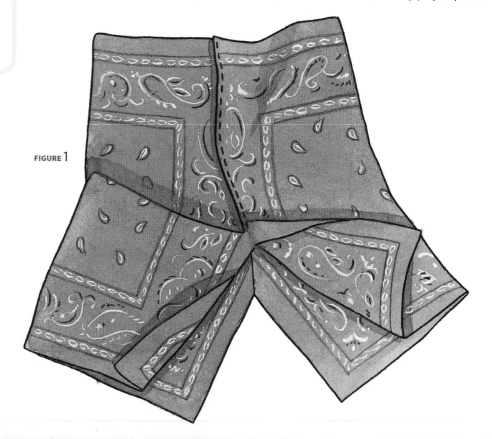

Baby Bib

When they're crafted with care, the most basic items take on a special significance—especially for those who may not have an easy way to wash clothes. This simple, thoughtfully embellished bib will meet the needs of both children and caregivers.

Designer: *Amanda Swan*

Hope Note

I am a Cambodian, born in Thailand's refugee camp. I was raised in Georgia since I was eight months old so I'd never experienced life outside of the United States. My parents took me back to Cambodia when I was 12 and it really opened my eyes to so much more in the world. So many humans needing just the little things, things we take for granted here.

Theary, Nebraska

Baby Bib

Basic Sewing Kit (page 124)

Bib template (page 131)

Bird, wing, and leaf templates (page 131)

1 fat quarter each of yellow, blue, red, and green print cotton

1 scrap of a different yellow print cotton

Paper-backed fusible web

All-purpose white, blue, yellow, red, and green sewing thread

Low-loft cotton batting

Hook-and-loop tape

Seam Allowance
¼ inch (6 mm), unless otherwise noted

1. Copy and enlarge the bib template on page 131, and cut it out. Pin the yellow and blue fabrics together with right sides facing. Lay the template on the fabrics, and cut through both layers. The blue will be the front of the bib, and the yellow will be the back.

> **TIP** Fat quarters come in handy for making small projects, patchwork, and appliqués. Typically, a quarter yard of fabric measures 9 x 44 inches (22.9 x 111.8 cm). A fat quarter is still a quarter yard of fabric, but it is a half yard of fabric that has been cut in half again to measure 18 x 22 inches (45.7 x 55.9 cm).

2. Trace the bird, wing, and leaf templates on page 131, and cut them out. Following the manufacturer's instructions, apply the paper-backed fusible web to the fabrics you will use for the appliqués: the bird from red fabric, the wing from green, and the leaf from the yellow scrap.

3. Lay the appliqué templates on the paper side of the fusible web that is attached to the fabrics. Trace around them, and cut them out. Peel away the paper backing on the fusible web.

4. Lay the bird on the bib front, positioning it in the lower right corner. Follow the manufacturer's instructions and press to adhere. Position the wing on the bird, and press to adhere. Position the leaf to the right of the bird's beak, and press to adhere.

5. Lay the bird on the bib front, positioning it in the lower right corner. Press to adhere. Position the wing on the bird, and press to adhere. Position the leaf to the right of the bird's beak, and press to adhere.

6. Zigzag around the edges of the appliqués. Use the blue thread around the bird, the red thread around the wing, and the yellow thread around the leaf.

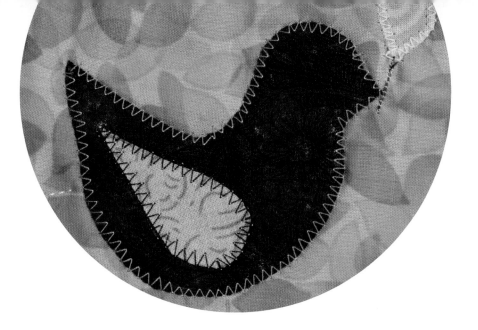

Charity

The Care Bags Foundation
www.carebags4kids.org

The Care Bags Foundation was started by an 11-year-old girl when she learned how many kids in crisis situations must leave their homes with very few of their own belongings. Over the years, the nonprofit has grown from a small home-based project helping a few kids in Iowa into a nationally recognized nonprofit organization that provides services to thousands of kids worldwide. Helped by volunteers and businesses, Care Bags creates and distributes beautiful fabric bags filled with essential and comforting items for disadvantaged children (newborn to 18 years old) around the world.

OTHER APPROPRIATE CHARITIES FOR THE BIB:

MotherLove Program (page 119)

Orphanages

Local women's and children's shelters

7. Using a straight stitch with green thread, sew a stem from the bottom of the leaf extending a little bit past the bird's beak.

8. Cut a 12-inch (30.5 cm) square from the batting, and lay it on your work surface. Lay the back of the bib right side up on the batting. Lay the blue front right side down on both layers. Align the edges of the front and back. Pin, and then sew around the edges through all layers, leaving a 3-inch (7.6 cm) opening along the bottom for turning. Trim the batting to shape.

9. Turn the bib right side out. Turn the edges of the opening into the seam allowance. Topstitch around the entire edge, making sure to stitch the opening closed, and press.

10. Using the white thread, use a straight stitch to machine quilt a line with double loops on the front at the right side of the bib's neck. If you prefer, hand quilt the line using a running stitch.

11. Cut a 1-inch (2.5 cm) strip from the hook-and-loop tape. Pin one side of the tape to the underside of the left bib neck. Pin the other side to the top side of the right bib neck. Sew each in place using a zigzag stitch and blue thread.

Designer: *Betsy Greer*

Fingerless Gloves

Functional, handsome, and suitable for both men and women, these fingerless gloves fit a wide range of hand sizes. They're easy to knit using wool yarn or any yarn that maintains the same gauge.

Approx 104 yd/94 m of **④** medium weight yarn

Size 4.5 mm (size 7 U.S.) pair of double-pointed needles

Stitch marker

Tapestry needle or crochet hook

Gauge
4.5 sts per inch (2.5 cm) using 4.5 mm (size 7 U.S.) needles

NOTE: The gloves are knit in the round in a k2, p2 ribbed pattern using double-pointed needles. The hole for the thumb is made by binding off stitches. See page 126 for knitting abbreviations and yarn weight chart.

1. CO 36 sts. Pm at the beginning of the first row.

2. K2, p2 in the round until the piece measures 8 inches (20.3 cm).

3. At the beginning of the next rnd, BO the first 6 sts, then continue k2, p2 until reaching the end of the rnd.

4. At the beginning of the following rnd, cast on 6 sts, then continue k2, p2 for the rest of the rnd. Continue in the k2, p2 ribbed pattern for another 1½ inches (3.8 cm). BO.

5. Weave in the end using the tapestry needle or crochet hook. Repeat to complete the pair.

The gloves were knit using 1 skein of Jo Sharp Silkroad Aran Tweed (85% Wool/10% Silk/5% Cashmere; 1.75oz/50g = 104yd/94m per skein).

Charity

The Yarnery's Mitten Fairy Project
www.yarnery.com

The Yarnery—a yarn shop that's been a fixture in Saint Paul, Minnesota, for more than 35 years—embraces community knitting projects. Minnesota winters can be brutally cold, and many children have to go to school each day without the proper outerwear to keep them warm. In response to this, The Yarnery initiated the Mitten Fairy Project. Each fall, the shop collects handknit mittens or gloves (along with scarves and hats) to distribute to children and teens in Saint Paul public schools. Check their website for collection dates and shipping information.

OTHER APPROPRIATE CHARITIES FOR THE GLOVES:

SOME (page 41)
Local winter clothing drives
Local homeless shelters

Hope Note

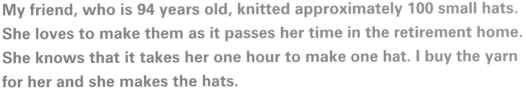

My friend, who is 94 years old, knitted approximately 100 small hats. She loves to make them as it passes her time in the retirement home. She knows that it takes her one hour to make one hat. I buy the yarn for her and she makes the hats.

Barbara, United States

Designer:
Maya Donenfeld

Backpack

Charities that serve many different causes often welcome backpacks. Made from a canvas drop cloth, this sturdy, washable knapsack will stand up to everyday use. Optional pockets can be added if you need a roomier pack.

Basic Sewing Kit (page 124)

Cotton canvas drop cloth

1 yard (.9 m) of lighter weight cotton for the lining and optional pocket

Elastic, ½ inch (1.3 cm) wide, for the inside pocket loops (optional)

65 inches (165.1 cm) of cotton webbing, 1 inch (2.5 cm) wide, for the straps

Thread of coordinating color

Seam Allowance
½ inch (1.3 cm), unless otherwise noted

Charity

Little Red Wagon Foundation
www.littleredwagonfoundation.com

The Little Red Wagon Foundation is an organization started in 2005 by eight-year-old Zach Bonner to help underprivileged kids. The nonprofit collects backpacks, toys, and school supplies for homeless children and kids in distress. In 2010, Zach (now 13) plans to walk from Tampa, Florida, to Los Angeles, California, to raise awareness of the more than 1.3 million homeless children living in the US. Please check the Little Red Wagon Foundation's website for other items needed.

OTHER APPROPRIATE CHARITIES FOR THE BACKPACK:

Literacy Volunteers of Atlanta (page 121)

Local schools

Local programs for foster children

What You Cut

Cotton Canvas
1 piece, 17 x 30 inches (43.2 x 76.2 cm)
1 circle, 9½ inches (24.1 cm) in diameter, for the bottom of the pack
1 piece, 12 x 18 inches (30.5 x 45.7 cm), for the inside pocket with loops (optional)

Lining
1 piece, 17 x 30 inches (43.2 x 76.2 cm)

1 circle, 9½ inches (24.1 cm) in diameter, for the bottom of the lining
1 piece, 9 x 10 inches (22.9 x 25.4 cm), for the outside patch pocket (optional)

Elastic
2 pieces, each 1 inch (2.5 cm) in length, for the inside pocket loops (optional)

Cotton Webbing
2 pieces, each 4 inches (10.2 cm) in length

---

1. Cut out all pieces. Set the remaining length of webbing aside.

2. Fold the larger rectangle cut from the lining in half widthwise with right sides together. Pin the ends together to make a tube, and sew. Press the seam open.

> **SIMPLIFY** Adding pockets takes more time but is well worth the effort. If you want to save a few steps, make a simple patch pocket described in steps 7–9 for the lining instead of the turned pocket described in steps 3–5.

3. Make the optional double pocket with loops for the inside of the pack. If you're not adding the pocket, go to step 6. Fold the smaller canvas rectangle in half widthwise with right sides together. With the fold at the top, stitch the sides and bottom, leaving

an opening of a couple of inches (5 cm) on the bottom for turning. Clip the corners and turn, making sure to push out all corners. Press the pocket, folding the raw edges of the opening into the seam allowance.

4. Topstitch the top edge of the pocket ½ inch (1.3 cm) from the fold. Pin the pocket right side up to the right side of the lining, centering the pocket on the seam. Make sure the top of the pocket is at least 4½ inches (11.4 cm) below the top of the lining in order to clear the stitching when you sew the casing for the straps.

5. Fold each elastic piece in half to make loops. Insert the raw edges of elastic in between the pocket and lining approximately 1 inch (2.5 cm) from the top of the pocket on each side, and pin in place. Topstitch the sides and bottom of the pocket ½ inch (1.3 cm) in from the edge, then edge stitch along the same edges. Backstitch several times at the top of the side seams to reinforce the pocket. If you want a double pocket, sew a straight line in the ditch of the seam down the center of the pocket. Turn the lining wrong side out.

6. Pin the circle cut from the lining to the bottom of the tube with right sides together. Sew around the circle using a ⅜-inch (9.5 mm) seam allowance. Notch the edge of the circle by cutting small V-shapes into the seam allowance, being careful to avoid cutting the stitching. Do not turn the lining; set aside.

7. Make the optional patch pocket for the outside of the pack. If you're not adding the pocket, go to step 10. Using the smaller rectangle cut from the lining fabric, hem one of the short ends by folding the fabric under ¾ inch (1.9 cm), and press. Sew the hem ½ inch (1.3 cm) in from the edge, and then edge stitch close to the fold. This is the top of the pocket.

8. Fold the sides and bottom of the pocket in ½ inch (1.3 cm), and press. Center the pocket on the length of the canvas rectangle opposite the seam. Make sure the top of the pocket is at least 4½ inches (11.4 cm) below one of the 30-inch (76.2 cm) sides, in order to clear the stitching when you sew the casing for the straps.

9. Stitch the sides and bottom of the pocket to the canvas. First topstitch ½ inch (1.3 cm) in from the edges of the pocket, and then edge stitch along the folds. Backstitch several times at the top of the side seams to reinforce the pocket.

10. As you did for the lining in step 2, fold the larger canvas rectangle in half widthwise with right sides together and raw edges aligned to make a tube. To leave an opening for the straps, measure 1 inch (2.5 cm) from the top of the seam, and pin to mark the spot. Then measure 1½ inches (3.8 cm) down from that point, and pin to mark the spot. Pin the remaining seam.

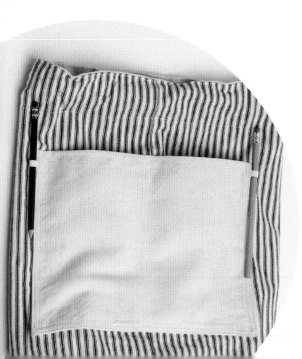

11. Begin stitching from the bottom of the seam. When you reach the pin at the 1½-inch (3.8 cm) mark, backstitch to lock your stitches, and cut the threads. Begin sewing again at the pin at the 1-inch (2.5 cm) mark. Backstitch to secure the threads, then continue sewing to close the seam.

12. Press the seam open. From the top edge, sew a 3-inch (7.6 cm) line of stitching approximately ½ inch (1.3 cm) from the seam line on both sides of the seam. Make sure to catch the seam allowance in the stitching.

13. Turn the canvas tube right side out. Lay the seam flat so you can easily see the opening you made in step 11. Reinforce the opening by using a tight zigzag or satin stitch directly above and below the opening (figure 1).

FIGURE 1

14. Turn the fabric inside out. Pin the canvas circle to the bottom as you did for the lining in step 6. Position the loops at the bottom of the bag. Measure 4 inches (10.2 cm) from each side of the bag's seam, and mark with pins. Fold the 4-inch (10.2 cm) lengths of webbing in half. Insert the loops in between the seam allowance so the loops will be on the outside of the bag. The raw edges of webbing should extend a bit from the seam allowance (figure 2).

15. Sew around the circle twice for extra strength using a ⅛-inch (9.5 mm) seam allowance. Backstitch over the webbing several times to reinforce the loops. Notch the curves along the edge of the circle.

16. Turn the canvas bag right side out. Make sure the lining is wrong side out. Tuck the canvas bag into the lining with right sides together.

17. Sew the two together at the top, leaving a 5-inch (12.7 cm) opening for turning. Turn the bag, tucking the lining inside. Fold the raw edges of the opening into the seam allowance, and pin. Edge stitch around the top of the bag through both layers.

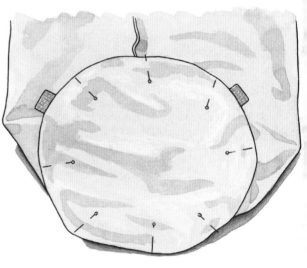

FIGURE 2

18. Stitch a line around the top of the bag to make a casing for the straps. Begin stitching at the bottom of the opening you made in steps 10 and 11, and stitch around the bag.

> **TIP:** To keep the line straight, attach a small piece of masking tape to your machine's throat plate to act as your stitching guide.

19. Attach a safety pin to the remaining length of webbing. Feed it through the opening and into the casing. Pull both ends until they're even. To prevent fraying, hem the ends of the webbing by folding them under ½ inch (1.3 cm), then once again before stitching. Slip each end of the strap into a bottom loop, and tie a knot. Note: The straps can be adjusted to the height of the child.

Designer: *Jhoanna Monte*

Sock Monkey

The perfect companion for anyone who needs a lift, this little critter will bring joy wherever he goes. The Craft Hope monkeys had personalities as varied as the argyle, polka-dotted, and striped socks from which they were made.

Basic Sewing Kit (page 124)

One pair of cotton socks, size large in a medium length

Felt scraps for the eyes and heart appliqué

⅛ yard (11.4 cm) of felt for the scarf

⅓ yard (30.5 cm) of fleece for the boy's vest

¼ yard (22.9 cm) of print cotton for the girl's skirt

Water-soluble fabric marker

Polyester fiberfill

Embroidery floss for hand stitching, and for the hair and facial features

Elastic, ¼ inch (6 mm) wide

Button (optional)

Seam Allowance
¼ inch (6 mm), unless otherwise noted

What You Cut

Felt
1 strip, ¾ x 14 inches (1.9 x 35.6 cm) for the scarf

Fleece
1 piece, 15 x 5 inches (38.1 x 12.7 cm) for the vest

Print Cotton
1 piece that is the measurement around the monkey's waist (W) plus 8 x 5 inches (W plus 20.3 x 12.7 cm) for the skirt. Note: Cut this after the monkey is stuffed to determine the waist measurement.

Charity

Operation Sock Monkey
www.operationsockmonkey.com

In an effort to inspire children with little to look forward to, Operation Sock Monkey places handmade sock monkeys with kids in need of some homemade love. In particular, the organization sends the sock monkeys to African children who have been affected by HIV/AIDS. They also work with Clowns Without Borders South Africa to provide laughter, hope, and healing to the children of these devastated communities.

OTHER APPROPRIATE CHARITIES FOR THE SOCK MONKEY:

Local hospital's pediatric unit

Local women's and children's shelters

Any child who needs a smile

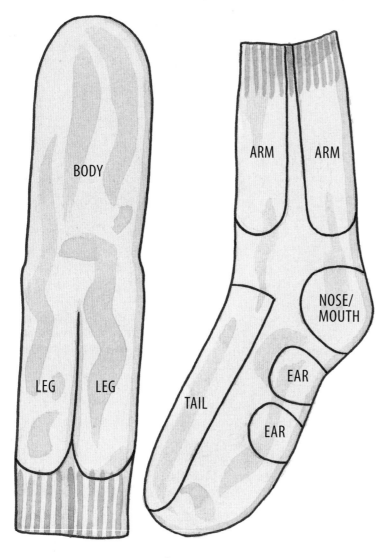

BODY

ARM   ARM

NOSE/
MOUTH

TAIL   EAR

EAR

LEG   LEG

FIGURE 1

Hope Note

I work in a kindergarten in Norway, and as our children have roots in many different countries in the world, I thought it would be great if we, too, as a kindergarten, did something for children less fortunate.

Eva, Norway

MONKEY

1. Refer to the illustration in figure 1. Turn both socks inside out and use the water-soluble fabric marker to draw the shapes on the socks as shown. Do not cut them out. Set aside. Note: One pair of socks makes one monkey.

2. Trace around a small coin twice on the felt scrap for the eyes, and cut them out. Draw a heart on the other felt scrap for the vest appliqué, and cut it out. Set aside. Note: If you think the monkey might be given to a young child, embroider the eyes instead of using felt scraps.

3. On the sock for the body and legs, sew around the dotted leg markings (figure 2) using a ¼-inch (6 mm) seam allowance. Leave a 1-inch (2.5 cm) opening as shown for turning and stuffing. Cut off the cuff (the top) of the sock, and lay aside. Cut the legs free by cutting on the solid lines marked for the legs.

4. Turn the body and legs of the monkey right side out. If needed, use a knitting needle to push out all the curves. Stuff the monkey, using small handfuls of the polyester fiberfill at a time. Work the stuffing down into both legs. Continue to stuff the monkey as firmly as possible. Note: Adjust the stuffing to allow the monkey to sit up on its own. Hand stitch the opening closed using the slip stitch (page 125).

5. Shape the neck. Measure approximately 4 inches (10.2 cm) down from the top of the monkey's head. Thread the needle with a long piece of the embroidery floss. Starting at the back, and leaving a 3-inch (7.6 cm) tail, weave the needle in and out around the monkey's neck to make gathering stitches. When you finish stitching, leave a 3-inch (7.6 cm) tail, and remove the needle. Pull both tails to gather the neck. Securely knot the floss at the back, and trim the loose ends.

6. Using the cuff (top) of the sock that you cut off in step 3, slip it over the monkey's head, like a turtleneck, to fit around the neck to hide the gathering stitches.

7. On the other sock, sew around the arms, tail, ears, and nose/mouth, as you did for the legs. When you sew around the nose/mouth, leave a small opening for turning and stuffing. Make sure to leave the tops of the arms and tail open for turning and stuffing. Cut the pieces out by cutting on the lines. For the ears, cut the folds along each straight edge to create an opening.

8. Turn the pieces right side out. If needed, use a knitting needle to push out all the curves. Use small handfuls of stuffing to stuff the arms and tail as firmly as possible. Turn the edges of each opening into the seam allowance. Use a slip stitch to hand stitch the openings closed.

9. Attach the arms to either side of the monkey just under the neck. Hand stitch, using a whipstitch or slip stitch (page 125). Attach the tail to the monkey's bottom. Hand stitch, using a slip stitch around the base of the tail.

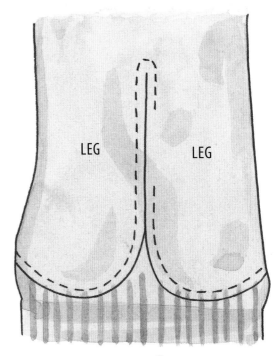

FIGURE 2

10. Use a small handful of stuffing to stuff the nose/mouth. Pin it to the monkey's head just above the neck. Using a slip stitch, hand stitch it firmly to the monkey's face. Before sewing it closed, add more stuffing until it's plump. Then stitch the opening closed.

11. Use embroidery floss to attach the eyes very securely to the monkey's face.

12. Sew the ears to either side of the monkey's head. Tuck the edges of each opening into the seam allowance, then hand stitch using a slip stitch to attach the ears very securely.

13. Use embroidery floss to hand stitch a long running stitch from the top of the head to define the hairline. Use embroidery floss to embroider eyebrows, a nose, and a mouth using small running stitches.

14. (Optional) Use a contrasting color of floss to embroider a small stitch in each eye, or use white fabric paint and add a small dot to each eye.

LITTLE HEROES PRESCHOOL BURN CAMP

The Craft Hope community contributed more than 240 sock monkeys to the Firefighters' Burn Institute's Little Heroes Burn Camp in Livermore, California. The Firefighter's Burn Institute was started by Sacramento firefighters in 1973 to support burn care, prevention, and recovery. Their preschool camp empowers burn survivors ages 3 to 6 years, and their families, to understand and cope with the physical and emotional challenges associated with burn recovery. The camp's counselors, nurses, activity directors, cooks, and drivers are all volunteers. The editors at Lark Crafts joined in the fun and made sock monkeys to send to the camp.

VEST

1. Cut the front and back of the vest. Fold the piece of fleece in half with the short edges aligned. Draw a trapezoid (figure 3) measuring 7½ x 5½ x 5 inches (19 x 14 x 12.7 cm). Cut through both layers. Set aside.

2. Appliqué the felt heart to one side of the front of the vest using a stitch of your choice.

3. Place the two pieces of the vest with right sides facing and sew them together, leaving the openings for the neck and arms (figure 4). Turn the vest right side out. Note: You won't need to finish the raw edges as fleece doesn't fray. Put the vest on the monkey by slipping it on at the legs. Pull the vest up, taking the arms through the armholes as you bring it up to the neck.

SKIRT

1. With right sides facing, fold the piece cut for the skirt in half widthwise, aligning the short edges, and sew. Hem the bottom edge by pressing it under ¼ inch (6 mm). Press under again ¼ inch (6 mm), and stitch.

2. Make the casing for the elastic. Press the top edge of the skirt under ¼ inch (6 mm). Press it under again ¾ inch (1.9 cm), and sew along the folded edge, approximately ½ inch (1.3 cm) from the top edge of the skirt. Leave a small opening for threading the elastic.

3. Cut a piece of the ¼-inch (6 mm) elastic to the monkey's waist measurement. Attach a small safety pin to one end. Thread it through the casing, sew the ends together, tuck it into the casing, and sew the casing closed.

SCARF

1. Make small cuts in both ends of the scarf strip to create fringed ends.

2. Wrap it around the monkey's neck, and hand stitch securely in place to keep the scarf from coming off. Use the button to decorate the scarf if you are sure the monkey will be given to a child over the age of three.

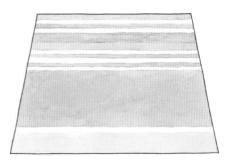

FIGURE 3

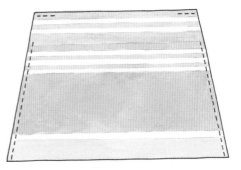

FIGURE 4

Designer: *Rebecca Ittner*

Natural Brown Sugar Soap

Shelters often request donations of handmade soaps, because they make the living quarters feel homier. With brown sugar, vanilla, and vitamin E oil, this soap is wonderfully simple to make. The recipe yields up to six bars.

1 pound (454 g) clear glycerin melt-and-pour soap

1½ tablespoons (22 g) brown sugar

1 teaspoon (5 mL) vitamin E oil

2 teaspoons (10 mL) vanilla essential oil

Large knife

Double boiler with lid

Measuring spoons

Metal spoon for stirring

4-cup (960 mL) glass measuring cup

Rubber spatula

Mold: plastic drawer organizer, 9 x 3 x 2 inches (22.9 x 7.6 x 5 cm)

Spray bottle filled with rubbing alcohol

Dough cutter or wavy cutter

1. Using the large knife, cut the soap into cubes, then, using the manufacturer's instructions, melt the soap in the double boiler, covering the double boiler with the lid.

2. Once the soap is melted, remove the double boiler from the heat, then add the brown sugar and vitamin E oil, stirring gently to incorporate.

3. Transfer the soap into the glass measuring cup using the rubber spatula, then stir in the essential oil. Pour the soap into the mold, then spray the surface of the soap with rubbing alcohol to eliminate any bubbles.

4. Allow the soap to cool and fully harden, then remove the soap from the mold. Using the dough cutter or wavy cutter, cut the soap into bars.

Charity

New Orleans Women's Shelter
www.nolawomenshelter.org

According to the National Coalition for the Homeless, New Orleans' rate of homelessness is more than four times that of most US cities. Since Hurricane Katrina, the number of the city's homeless has nearly doubled. Women and children under the age of eight make up the greatest proportion of individuals without a home. New Orleans Women's Shelter was founded to respond to this need. It strives to change the trajectory of homeless women's lives by providing them with support and access to living wage jobs, banking services, and educational and parenting classes. The majority of the residents in the shelter, located in the Upper 9th Ward, live there for three to six months until they are ready to transition to private housing or independent living. The shelter prefers attractive bars of soap (instead of samples or hotel extras) to help create a sense of home, rather than transience, for their families. They've also asked for craft supplies (especially beading) for the women and children.

OTHER APPROPRIATE CHARITIES FOR THE SOAP:

Local homeless shelters

Local nursing homes

Any friend or neighbor going through a hard time

Designer: *Maya Donenfeld*

Baby Kimonos

Made from soft cotton flannel, this project offers warmth, comfort, and special features, including fold-over sleeve cuffs that will protect a baby from accidental scratches. Two pattern variations let you choose between elasticized or envelope openings at the kimono's bottom.

Basic Sewing Kit (page 124)

Template (page 130)

Craft paper

1½ yards (1.3 m) of cotton flannel or jersey knit or two XL or XXL T-shirts

1 yard (.9 m) of ribbon or twill tape

16 inches (40.6 cm) of elastic, ½ inch (1.3 cm) wide

Seam Allowance
⅜ inch (9.5 mm), unless otherwise noted

NOTE: These white gowns are beautiful, but depending on your charity, you may want to use a darker, more practical, fabric.

1. Copy, enlarge, and cut out the templates on page 130. Trace them onto craft paper, and cut them out.

2. Pin the pattern pieces to the fabric, and cut. Note: Make sure you cut a left front and right front. If you're using jersey knit from a T-shirt, make sure the stretch of the fabric runs parallel to the bottom hem. Do not open the envelope and cuffs; keep them folded as cut.

3. Lay the back piece right side up on your work surface. Note: If you're making the version with the envelope, lay the folded envelope on top of the back piece with the raw edges aligned. The fold will be facing toward the top of the garment. Lay the front pieces, right side down and one on top of the other, over the back piece (and envelope, if applicable). Pin the pieces together through all layers along the shoulders, sleeves, and sides.

4. At the end of each sleeve, sandwich a cuff between the front and the back of the sleeve with raw edges aligned. The fold will be facing in toward the center of the sleeve.

Charity

Giving Children Hope
www.gchope.org

Giving Children Hope is a grassroots, faith-based organization dedicated to alleviating poverty domestically and abroad through disaster relief, health and community development, vocational training, and advocacy. GCHope helps to better develop under-resourced clinics, hospitals, and orphanages. It connects indigenous community leaders in need of resources with grassroots efforts around the world to secure and deliver supplies. The organization strives to listen to a community's needs instead of imposing its ideas or strategy on the community, believing "a project has the greatest chance for success when the community has true ownership and input." Giving Children Hope's website lists other items needed for their work helping Haitians recover from the earthquake.

OTHER APPROPRIATE CHARITIES FOR THE BABY KIMONOS:

MotherLove Program (page 119)

Youth Action International (page 49)

Any aid group working with orphanages

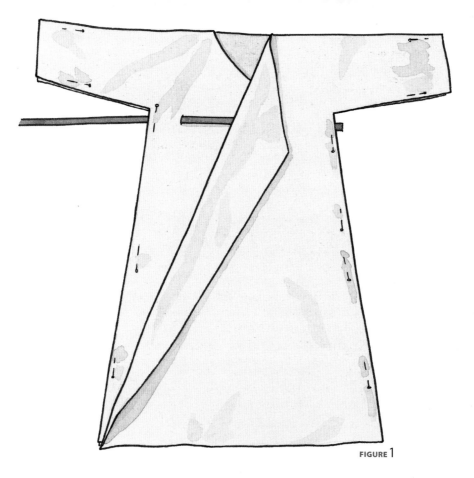

FIGURE 1

5. Cut the ribbon or twill tape into four pieces, each 9 inches (22.9 cm) long. Set two of the pieces aside. Slip the end of one ribbon into the seam allowance just below the armpit, and pin in place. Slip the other ribbon in between the two fronts, tucking one end in the seam allowance just below the armpit, and pin in place (figure 1).

6. Sew all the seams, curving the underarm seam as you sew around the armpit. Clip the underarm curves, making sure to avoid cutting the stitches. Use a zigzag or over-cast stitch on the seam allowances to prevent fraying.

7. Finish the front flaps and neckline. Start at the corner of one of the front flaps. Fold the edge of the fabric under ¼ inch (6 mm), and press. Work all the way around the neckline until you get to the corner on the other front flap. Then turn the edge under again ¼ inch (6 mm), pressing and pinning as you go. Note: Be careful to avoid stretching the fabric as you work.

8. As you did for the neckline, turn, press, and pin the straight edges on each front flap. Place and pin the remaining ribbons in the pressed hems at the corner on each front flap before sewing (figure 2).

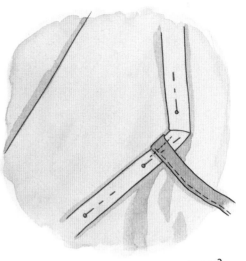

FIGURE 2

9. Starting at the bottom of one front flap, topstitch ¼ inch (6 mm) in from the edge. Sew all the way up and around the neckline and down the other flap.

10. Turn the garment right side out, and lay it flat on your work surface. Tie all ribbons (figure 3). Pin the front flaps in place, making sure each of the flaps is as close to the side seams as possible. Turn the garment inside out.

11. If you're making the version with the envelope bottom, simply sew the bottom closed by stitching through all layers. If you're making the version with the gathered elastic bottom, make a casing: fold the hem over ¾ inch (1.9 cm), and zigzag it along the raw edge. Leave a 1-inch (2.5 cm) opening for threading the elastic. Attach a safety pin to one end of the elastic, and feed it through the casing. Sew the ends of the elastic together, and then sew the opening closed.

12. Hem the ends of the sleeves. Turn the edge over ½ inch (1.3 cm), then zigzag along the raw edge through all layers. Repeat for the other sleeve. Note: The hems will be thicker where you have the two extra layers of the cuff. Turn the garment right side out, and fold the cuffs over the end of each sleeve.

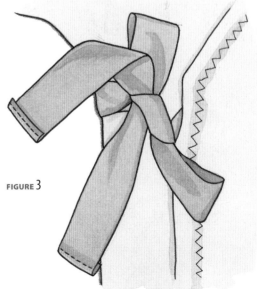

FIGURE 3

Designer: *Rebekah Williams*

Soft Blocks & Balls

Soft blocks and balls can be used by organizations working with toddlers to help develop hand-eye coordination. They are also a great way to put fabric scraps to good use. Amy Butler donated fabric from her August Fields collection for this project.

Basic Sewing Kit (page 124)

Template (page 128)

Cotton print fabric scraps, none smaller than 10 inches (25.4 cm) square

Water-soluble fabric marker

Hypoallergenic polyester fiberfill

BLOCK

1. Choose three coordinating fabric scraps. Cut two 5-inch (12.7 cm) squares from each fabric for a total of six squares.

2. Draw your sewing line: using the water-soluble fabric marker on the wrong side of the fabric, measure and draw a line ½ inch (1.3 cm) in from all four sides of each square. Draw the lines to the edge of the fabric so they cross at the corners.

3. Lay out the fabric squares in a cross design (figure 1), arranging the prints in a pleasing manner.

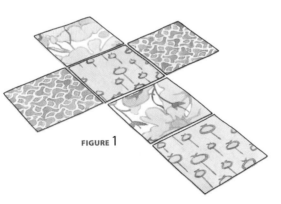

FIGURE 1

4. With right sides together, pin the top square to the one beneath it. Start and stop sewing where the lines intersect at the corners, backstitching at the beginning and end of the seam. Note: Do not stitch beyond the intersection of the lines. This will make turning your cube much easier.

5. Continue sewing the adjacent squares together, as in step 4, down the straight line of your cross until it is finished. Then sew the two side squares on one at a time. Press the seams flat.

6. Begin forming the cube by sewing the sides with right sides together. Continue until all but one side of your cube is left to sew.

Charity

Miracle Foundation
www.miraclefoundation.org

The Miracle Foundation is dedicated to empowering children in India to reach their full potential, one orphan at a time. The organization renovates existing orphanages, builds new ones, and finds sponsors for the children in the orphanages. Along with working to provide healthy food, tuition, better living conditions, clothing, and medical care, the nonprofit also provides each child with love, affection, and hope for a bright future. Craft Hope participants from around the world made close to 4,000 blankets, beanies, and booties for the children the Miracle Foundations serves. Their orphanages have now asked for soft balls and blocks to aid in some of the developmental games they play with the babies and toddlers.

OTHER APPROPRIATE CHARITIES FOR THE BLOCKS AND BALLS:

MotherLove Program (page 119)

Giving Children Hope (page 69)

Any orphanage

7. On the remaining side, stitch in from each edge, leaving a 2-inch (5 cm) opening for turning and stuffing. Note: Backstitch on each side of the opening to reinforce it, as stuffing the block will place stress on the seams. Carefully trim the excess fabric at the corners.

8. Turn the cube right side out. Stuff with the polyester fiberfill until the cube is firm. Use small amounts of stuffing at a time. Make sure to press it firmly into the corners. Hand stitch the opening closed.

BALL

1. Choose three coordinating fabrics. Trace and cut out the pattern piece on page 128. Cut two pieces from each fabric for a total of six pieces.

2. Make the first half of the ball. Think of assembling it from two pairs of three fabric pieces each. To begin, stitch one edge of two pieces together, right sides facing, using a ½-inch (1.3 cm) seam allowance. Fold the seam allowance back when you add the third piece, so you can see where the angles of the pieces align. Repeat with the remaining three pieces, keeping the prints in the same order.

3. Pin the two halves of the ball with right sides together. Be sure to carefully line up the points at the top and bottom where the three pieces meet on each half. Stitch the halves together, leaving a 2-inch (5.1 cm) opening at the center of one of the seams for turning and stuffing. Note: Backstitch on each side of the opening to reinforce it, as stuffing the ball will place stress on the seams. Carefully trim the excess fabric at the corners.

4. Turn the ball right side out. Stuff with the fiberfill until firm. Hand stitch the opening closed.

Hope Note

I just can't tell you how much we appreciate all of the amazing handmade items for the orphans. I can't believe how many we received and how many people stepped up to the plate to take care of these kids! They are so lucky to have people in the world like this.

Caroline, Texas (Founder of the Miracle Foundation)

Red Fleece Mittens

Warm hands, warm heart! Designed with snug elastic wrists, these extra-long polar fleece mittens will keep out the cold. And because fleece doesn't unravel, sewing them is easy.

Mitten Designer: *Amanda Carestio*
Embroidery Designer: *Aimee Ray*

Hope Note

I feel like part of something immense and precious and hope that it brings warmth and smiles.

Ana, Leganes, Spain

Red Fleece Mittens

Basic Sewing Kit (page 124)

Mitten template (page 127)

Embroidery template (page 127)

¼ yard (22.9 cm) of red fleece

Tracing paper

Embroidery floss and needle

Red thread

40 inches (101.6 cm) of round elastic cord

Seam Allowance
½ inch (1.3 cm), unless otherwise noted

1. Copy and enlarge the mitten and embroidery templates on page 127, and cut them out. Fold the fabric in half lengthwise with selvages aligned. Center the pattern on the fleece, and cut through both layers to yield two mitten shapes. Flip the pattern over, and cut two more mitten shapes.

2. Trace the embroidery design from the template onto tracing paper. Pin the paper patterns securely in place to the front of each mitten. Refer to the photo for the floss colors to use for each motif. Embroider the designs through the tracing paper and top layer of each mitten using the backstitch.

3. Tear away the tracing paper. Note: You may need to use a needle or tweezers to pull out the pieces from underneath your stitches.

4. Pin the mitten shapes together with right sides facing. Using a ¼-inch (6 mm) seam allowance, stitch around the outside edge of the shape, leaving the bottom edge open.

5. Cut off the excess seam allowance, especially around the thumb. Be careful to avoid cutting the stitches.

6. Hem the mittens while they're still inside out. Fold the bottom edge up 1 inch (2.5 cm), pin, and then stitch around the hemline. Note: You may find it easier to hem the mittens before stitching them together.

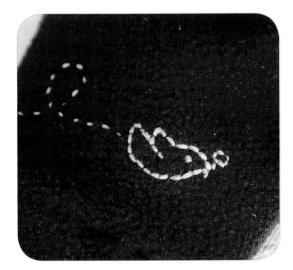

7. Turn the mittens right side out. Snip a small hole near the outside bottom edge of each mitten, cutting only through the top layer of the hem. Note: Fleece will not unravel, so you don't have to worry that the openings will fray.

8. Cut the length of elastic cord in half. Attach a safety pin to one end of one piece of the elastic cord. Thread the cord through the hole, around the hemline casing of the mitten, and out through the same hole.

9. Pull the cord taut to lightly gather the edge of the mitten. Tie the ends into a double-knotted bow. Repeat steps 8 and 9 for the other mitten.

Charity

LOWO Child and Family Services
www.friendsofpineridgereservation.org/organizations/LOWO.shtml

The Lakota Oyate Wakanyeja Owicakiyapi (LOWO) Child and Family Services Agency, situated on the Pine Ridge Reservation in South Dakota, provides child and family services, specifically focused on children who come from abusive and neglectful situations. LOWO supports comprehensive, culturally appropriate services that meet the basic needs of Lakota families, incorporating Lakota cultural beliefs, philosophy, traditions, and ceremonies as an important basis for helping children and families strengthen their identity as tribal people.

OTHER APPROPRIATE CHARITIES FOR THE MITTENS:

SOME (page 41)

Local homeless shelters

Local winter clothing drives

Designer: *Geninne D. Zlatkis*

Thank-You Cards & Stamp

The parents of sick children often want to express their gratitude to healthcare workers, volunteers, family members, and friends. These delightful notecards will make it easy for them to send thanks to the people who've eased their burdens. Use the template provided to carve the bird stamp, or design your own pattern.

Soft-lead pencil

Bird and flower templates (page 128)

Tracing paper or a sheet of vellum

4-inch square (10.2 cm) rubber-stamp carving block

Bone folder or small spoon

Linoleum cutter with number 1 and 5 tips

Craft knife

2 ink pads in contrasting colors

Purchased card blanks and envelopes

1. Using the soft-lead pencil, trace all the lines of the bird and flower templates (page 128) onto the tracing paper or vellum.

2. Lay the tracings on the rubber-stamp carving block with the pencil lines facing the rubber. Make sure both designs fit on the block.

3. Rub the back of the tracing paper or vellum with the bone folder or back of a small spoon. Rub until all the lines of the images have been transferred onto the carving block. Once you're done with this step, lift the tracing paper and discard.

4. Insert the number 1 (thinnest) tip into the handle of the linoleum cutter. Carve out all the lines of the bird and flower designs that are on the rubber block.

> **TIP** Follow these handy tips for cutting the block. Don't jab the block when cutting; instead, slide the linoleum cutter on the block as if it were a little shovel. Always carve away from yourself, and be extremely careful because the tips are very sharp. When you need to change cutting directions, rotate the block.

Charity

Starlight Children's Foundation
www.starlight.org/crafthope

For 25 years, Starlight Children's Foundation has been dedicated to helping seriously ill children and their families cope with their pain, fear, and isolation through entertainment, education, and family activities. Starlight's programs have been proven to distract children from their pain, help them better understand and manage their illnesses, and connect families facing similar challenges so that no one feels alone. Through a network of chapters and offices, Starlight provides ongoing support to children, parents, and siblings in all states in the U.S. and in the Canadian provinces with an array of outpatient, hospital-based, and Internet offerings. Programs are also delivered internationally through affiliates in Australia, Japan, and the United Kingdom.

OTHER APPROPRIATE CHARITIES FOR THE STAMPED CARDS:

MD Anderson Cancer Center (page 103)

Alex's Lemonade Stand (page 95)

Orphan Foundation of America (page 29)

5. After you have finished cutting out all of the lines of the bird and flower, remove the number 1 tip from the handle and insert the number 5 tip (widest). Cut around the bird and flower design to outline them (figure 1).

6. Use the craft knife to cut out the two figures using the outline you made in step 5 as your guide. Discard the leftover trimmings from the rubber block.

7. Use the number 5 tip to clean out the outer edges of your stamp. Go back over the design with the number 1 tip to clean out all of the nooks and crannies, such as in between the bird's claws.

8. When you're finished carving, wash your stamps with warm water and soap to clean out any crumbs of rubber left behind. Pat dry, then let them air dry for a couple of minutes before inking them.

9. To ink your stamps, place them facing up on your work surface, and apply the ink with the pad facing down. Pat the stamp until it is completely and uniformly covered with ink.

10. Make a few test prints on a white sheet of paper. If there are any parts of the stamp that you forgot to carve out, it will show up at this point, and you can go back with the cutter and make adjustments.

11. When you are satisfied with the results of your test prints, clean your work area, making sure your work surface is flat and free of any debris. Lay the card blanks facing up. Stamp the bird first and then stamp the flower on his beak.

12. (Optional) Use the flower stamp to stamp the back flap of the envelope as well.

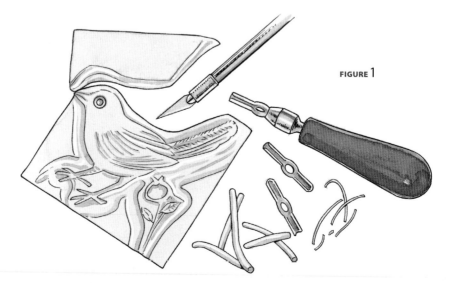

FIGURE 1

Stenciled T-Shirt

T-shirts for boys and girls are one of the items many nonprofits need the most. This stenciled design makes it easy to create multiple shirts with the help of a few volunteers. Once you're done, send the shirts off along with other much-needed items like socks, underwear, and toiletry supplies.

Designer: *Blair Stocker*

Stenciled T-Shirt

Basic Sewing Kit (page 124)

Template (page 129)

Cotton T-shirt in white or light color

Freezer paper

Craft knife with cutting mat

Fabric paint in any color

Paintbrush or sponge

Paper-backed fusible web

Cotton print fabric scraps in green and brown for the acorns

Embroidery floss to coordinate with the acorns

Embroidery needle

1. Prewash the T-shirt, dry it, press it, and set it aside.

2. Copy, enlarge, and trace the template on page 129. Make two tracings of it on separate pieces of the freezer paper. Note: Trace the template on the dull side—not the waxy side—of the paper.

3. Place the traced paper on the cutting mat, and use the craft knife to carefully cut out the motifs. On one stencil, only cut away the branch. On the other stencil, only cut away the leaves.

4. Preheat your iron on the cotton setting with no steam. Make sure the T-shirt is right side out before laying it flat on your ironing surface. Place a plain piece of the freezer paper, waxy side up, inside the shirt between the front and back. Position it approximately where you'll be painting your stencil. Lightly press the top of the shirt. The paper will adhere to the fabric and keep the paint from seeping through to the back of the shirt.

5. Place your stencil with the cut branch waxy side down on the front of the shirt. Lightly press in place. Move the shirt to a protected work surface for painting.

6. Dip the paintbrush or sponge in the fabric paint. Using a straight up and down motion, apply the paint by dabbing it on the stencil. Do not apply the paint in back and forth brushstrokes. Allow the paint to dry thoroughly before gently peeling away the stencil.

7. As you did in step 5, adhere the second stencil with the cut leaves to the shirt. Be careful to line up the stencil with the design that is already painted. Follow the instructions in step 6 for painting the stencil. Allow to dry.

8. Make the acorn appliqués: Following the manufacturer's instructions, apply the paper-backed fusible web to the fabrics you will use for the acorns. Trace the acorns from the template on page 129, and cut them out. Lay the acorn patterns on the paper side of the fusible web that is attached to the fabrics. Trace around them, and cut them out.

9. Peel away the paper backing on the fusible web. Position the acorns on the shirt following the placement on the template. Follow the manufacturer's instructions to adhere them to the T-shirt.

10. Embroider the front: Hand stitch the acorns using the embroidery floss and needle. Use a running stitch around all of the acorns and tops to help secure the appliqués to the shirt. Embroider veins on the leaves using a running stitch.

11. Allow the shirt to dry flat overnight, then follow manufacturer's instructions on the fabric paint for heat setting. Once this is done, the shirt should wash perfectly and hold up well.

> **TIP** Why restrict yourself to the colors of nature? Try different color schemes for the branch, leaves, and acorns. And remember, white shirts are cool for hot climates, but darker colors may be more practical for children where access to laundry is an issue.

BEYOND THE BEACH
Children's Foundation

Charity

Beyond the Beach Children's Foundation
www.beyondthebeach.ca

Beyond the Beach's mission is to encourage travelers to make their journeys more than just vacations by reaching beyond the beach to help equip the children of The Dominican Republic with the tools necessary for learning, living, dreaming, and achieving. The foundation seeks to empower the children to free themselves from the restraints of poverty and lack of opportunity, so they can decide their own futures. The non-profit hopes visitors to The Dominican Republic will save a bit of room in their suitcases in order to bring needed items—school supplies and new or gently used clean children's clothes—for the local youth. You can also mail items to the foundation at the mailing address found at www.beyondthebeach.ca/crafthope.

OTHER APPROPRIATE CHARITIES FOR T-SHIRTS:

Youth Action International (page 49)
SOME (page 41)
Local homeless shelters

Designer: *Molly Dunham*

Art Kit

Children everywhere will appreciate this cheerful collection of art supplies. The elastic pencil holder and side pocket for finished drawings are just two of the nifty features of this foldable cloth pouch.

Charity

The Preemptive Love Coalition
www.preemptivelove.org

A nonprofit that believes in healing hearts with love, The Preemptive Love Coalition works to provide life-saving heart surgery to thousands of Iraqi children. To promote a culture in which Iraqis engage in their own advancement rather than accept handouts, PLC asks parents of children seeking heart surgery to contribute toward the cost of their child's care. When the patient's family can't contribute out of their own personal savings, they're encouraged to appeal to extended family, friends, employers, and religious communities for financial help. PLC then seeks the additional needed funding from local charities, businesses, and philanthropists. Through sharing the responsibility for funding these surgeries, the organization hopes to nurture the values of volunteerism and cooperation that will eventually produce a greater love for everyone in the community while providing more local funding to solve local problems.

OTHER APPROPRIATE CHARITIES FOR THE ART KIT:

Alex's Lemonade Stand (page 95)

New Orlean's Women's Shelter (page 67)

Pediatric unit of a local hospital

Basic Sewing Kit (page 124)

¼ yard (22.9 cm) of fabric for the kit exterior

¼ yard (22.9 cm) of fabric for the kit interior

¼ yard (22.9 cm) of fusible interfacing

¼ yard (22.9 cm) of elastic, ¾ inch (1.9 cm) wide

¼ yard (22.9 cm) of elastic, ½ inch (1.3 cm) wide

Coordinating thread

Tailor's chalk

8 mini colored pencils

Blank notepad, 4 x 6 inches (10.2 x 15.2 cm)

Seam Allowance
½ inch (1.3 cm), unless otherwise noted

What You Cut

Exterior Fabric
1 piece, 14½ x 7½ inches (36.8 x 19 cm)

Interior Fabric
3 pieces, each 7½ x 5½ inches (19 x 14 cm), for the panels
1 piece, 6½ x 5½ inches (16.5 x 14 cm), for the notebook pocket
1 piece, 7½ x 4 inches (19 x 10.2 cm), for the pocket for drawings

Fusible Interfacing
1 piece, 14½ x 7½ inches (36.8 x 19 cm)
1 piece, 7½ x 5½ inches (19 x 14 cm)

Elastic
Cut one piece from each of the elastics, each 7½ inches (19 cm) long

---

1. Following the manufacturer's instructions, apply the larger piece of fusible interfacing to the wrong side of the piece cut for the kit exterior. In the same way, apply the smaller piece of interfacing to the wrong side of one of the 7½ x 5½-inch (19 x 14 cm) pieces cut for the panels.

2. Make the first panel: Center the wider piece of elastic, with raw ends aligned, on the 7½ x 5½-inch (19 x 14 cm) piece with the interfacing. Stitch along the short edges of the panel to hold the elastic in place using a ¼-inch (6 mm) seam allowance.

Hope Note

Please count me in. I would love to make a tiny difference in this world. Especially in a kid's world.

Mina, Brazil

3. Mark and stitch the elastic to make the loops for the colored pencils: Measure 1½ inches (3.8 cm) in from each end of the elastic, and mark the points with the tailor's chalk. From one of these marks, measure and mark the elastic at ¾-inch (1.9 cm) intervals, stopping when you reach the other 1½-inch (3.8 cm) mark. Stitch across the elastic at all marks, backstitching to lock in place. Set this panel aside.

4. Make the pocket to hold the notepad on the second panel: On the 6½ x 5½-inch (16.5 x 14 cm) piece cut for the pocket, fold one of the short ends under ¼ inch (6 mm), and press. Fold under again ¼ inch (6 mm), press, and then topstitch ⅛ inch (3 mm) in from the edge.

5. Place this piece on top of a 7½ x 5½-inch (19 x 14 cm) panel piece, both with right sides up. Align the raw edges, and stitch the pocket to the panel using a ¼-inch (6 mm) seam allowance. Set aside.

6. Make the pocket to hold the finished drawings on the third panel: On the 7½ x 4-inch (19 x 10.2 cm) piece cut for the pocket, fold the long left edge under ¼ inch (6 mm), and press. Fold the edge under again ¼ inch (6 mm), press, and then topstitch ⅛ inch (3 mm) in from the edge.

7. Place this piece on top of the remaining 7½ x 5½-inch (19 x 14 cm) panel piece, both with right sides up, aligning the raw edges along the top, bottom, and right side. Lay the remaining piece of elastic on the panel, placing it 1½ inches (3.8 cm) away from the edge of the pocket. Stitch along the short edges of the panel to hold the elastic in place using a ¼-inch (6 mm) seam allowance.

8. Pin and then stitch the three panels together on their long sides: The panel with the elastic loops will be at the left, the panel with the notebook pocket will be in the center, and the panel with the pocket for the finished drawings will be at the right (figure 1). Press the seams open.

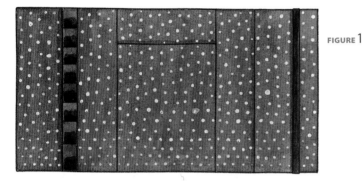

FIGURE 1

9. Lay the exterior piece right side up on your work surface. Lay the pieced interior on top of it with right sides facing. Pin them together along the edges, leaving a 4½-inch (11.4 cm) opening along the right side for turning, then stitch.

10. Clip each corner, being careful to avoid cutting the stitches. Turn the pouch right side out, and use a knitting needle to push out all corners. Turn the edges of the opening into the seam allowance, and press the entire kit. Pin the opening together.

11. Topstitch around the kit ⅛ inch (3 mm) in from the edges. Note: Do not topstitch the ½-inch (1.3 cm) elastic on the third panel. Begin topstitching in the upper right-hand corner of the interior of the kit, just to the left of the ½-inch (1.3 cm) elastic. Hold the elastic out of the way and to the right of the needle as you stitch the top right corner, down the right side, and along the bottom right corner of the kit.

12. Place the eight colored pencils in the elastic loops and the pad of paper in the middle pocket. Fold the side with the pencils over the center panel, then fold the other panel over them, using the elastic on that panel to close the kit.

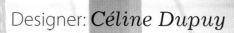

Designer: *Céline Dupuy*

Smocked Dress

A great technique if you're making garments for girls of various sizes, smocking is simpler than it looks! Follow the easy project instructions, and your dress will be a success.

Basic Sewing Kit (page 124)

1¾ yards (1.6 m) of print cotton

White elastic thread

White cotton thread

Seam Allowance
½ inch (1.3 cm), unless otherwise noted

1. From the print cotton, cut one rectangle, 24 x 60 inches (61 x 152.4 cm) for the dress, and two strips, each 1¾ x 12 inches (4.4 x 30.5 cm), for the straps. Note: This pattern makes a dress for a five- to six-year-old child with a chest measurement of 24 inches (61 cm). To size for all ages, multiply the child's chest measurement by 2½ to determine the total length of fabric to cut. This will give you the extra fabric you need to accommodate the gathers for the machine smocking.

2. Fold the rectangle in half widthwise, wrong sides facing, with the two short ends aligned. Pin along the edge. Make a French seam: Sew the first seam on the right side of the fabric. Trim the seam allowance to ⅛ inch (3 mm). Press the seam to one side. Turn the piece inside out, and press along the seam. Make the second seam on the wrong side of the fabric to encase the first seam by stitching in from the edge using a ¼-inch (6 mm) seam allowance.

3. Hem the top and bottom edges: On each, turn the edge under ½ inch (1.3 cm), and press. Turn the edge under again ½ inch (1.3 cm), and press. Stitch to finish the hem.

4. Prepare the machine for smocking: Loosely wind a bobbin by hand with the elastic thread, being careful to avoid stretching the elastic as you wind. Thread your upper machine with the cotton thread.

Charity

Youth Action International
www.youthactioninternational.org

Youth Action International was founded by Liberian activist Kimmie Weeks. At age 16, Weeks released a groundbreaking report on and lobbied for the disarmament of approximately 20,000 Liberian child soldiers. This defiant act resulted in assassination attempts. After he was granted political asylum in the United States, he started the nonprofit. Youth Action International is a network of young international leaders working to rebuild war-torn African communities. Using local materials and employing local people, YAI maximizes the economic and social impact of its programs, which include building schools, starting vocational training centers, and micro-lending. For more information on YAI, see page 49.

OTHER APPROPRIATE CHARITIES FOR THE SMOCKED DRESS:

Children of the Forest (page 93)

ORPHANetwork (page 31)

Pan de Vida (page 17)

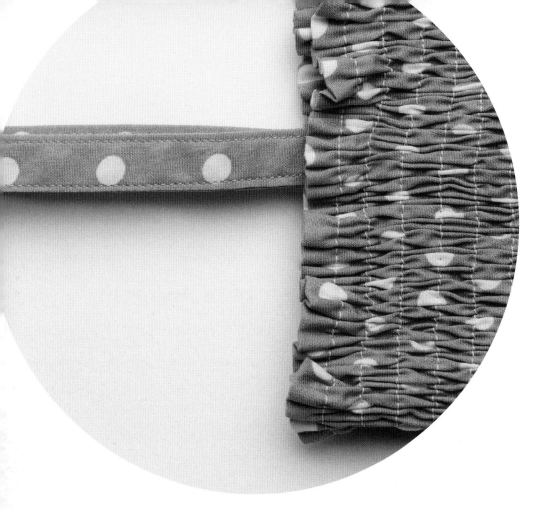

5. Starting at the back seam, stitch around the upper part of the dress to create 11 rows of elasticized smocking. Backstitch at the beginning and the end of each row. After you sew the first row, use it as your guide to stitch the next row by placing the right side of the presser foot next to it. Continue in this way until you have a total of 11 rows.

6. Make the straps: Fold a strip in half lengthwise with wrong sides facing, and press. Then fold each long edge into the middle to align with the center fold. Press, and then unfold the strip. Press each of the short ends under ¼ inch (6 mm). Refold the strip, and press. Topstitch the open long edge ⅛ inch (3 mm) in from the fold, and press. Repeat for the other strap. Sew the straps to the dress by hand.

Ruffled Pillowcase Skirt

Made of cool, lightweight fabric, pillowcases provide the perfect material for projects going to hot climates. The adjustable drawstring waist of this skirt makes it suitable for girls of all sizes. Use patterned or solid-colored pillowcases to create skirts in different styles.

Designer:
Christina Carleton

Ruffled Pillowcase Skirt

Basic Sewing Kit (page 124)	Elastic, ½ inch (1.3 cm) wide
Two washed pillowcases in identical or coordinating prints	Ribbon (optional), ½ inch (1.3 cm) wide
	Seam Allowance
Rotary cutter with cutting mat	½ inch (1.3 cm), unless otherwise noted

1. Calculate the measurements for the skirt: Width will be the widest point at the hips, plus 6 inches (15.2 cm). The length will be the desired finished length, measured from low on the waist, plus 3¾ inches (9.5 cm).

2. Use the width and length to determine the dimensions of each tier: For the top tier, the measurement will be the width by the length measurement minus 7½ inches (19 cm). The second tier will be a strip that is the width measurement by 4½ inches (11.4 cm). The third tier (the ruffle) will be a strip that is the width measurement plus 3 inches (7.6 cm) by 1½ inches (3.8 cm).

> **NOTE:** If you prefer a more substantial hem, which may give the ruffle more body, increase the length of the third tier during cutting.

3. Turn the pillowcases inside out. On each, cut the long edges (one seam and one fold), leaving the shortest seam at the top intact. Square the newly cut edges, using the grid on the cutting mat as your guide, and trim the excess with the rotary cutter.

4. Make sure each pillowcase is folded right side out on the remaining short seam. Lay them on your work surface with the seams facing left. The seams will become one of the side seams of the skirt. Divide your width measurement in half, and cut the tiers (figure 1). Note: In some cases, it might be necessary to sew strips together to get your required width.

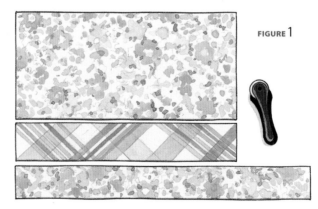

FIGURE 1

5. Unfold the tiers at the seams to open them full width. Pin the second tier to the bottom edge of the first tier, with right sides together and seams aligned, and sew. Trim the seam to ¼ inch (6 mm), and zigzag the edge to prevent fraying. Press the seam toward the second tier. On the right side, topstitch ⅛ inch (3 mm) down from the seam line.

6. With right sides together and raw edges aligned, pin the remaining side seam of the skirt together, and sew. Trim the seam to ¼ inch (6 mm), and zigzag the edge to prevent fraying.

7. Make and attach the ruffle: With right sides together, sew the short ends of the ruffle to make a loop. Trim the seam to ¼ inch (6 mm), and zigzag the edge to prevent fraying. Hem the ruffle. First, zigzag along the bottom edge to prevent fraying. Then turn and press the zigzagged edge under ⅛ to ¼ inch (3 to 6 mm), and sew.

8. Run a gathering stitch ¼ inch (6 mm) in from the raw edge of the ruffle. With right sides together and raw edges aligned, align the side seams of the ruffle with the side seams of the skirt, and pin. Gather the ruffle to the skirt, evenly adjusting the gathers on the front and back.

9. Sew the ruffle to the skirt: Trim the seam to ¼ inch (6 mm), and zigzag the edge to prevent fraying. Press the seam up. On the right side, topstitch ⅛ inch (3 mm) up from the seam line.

> **NOTE:** To make an elastic waist, follow steps 10-11. To make a drawstring ribbon waist, follow steps 12-14.

10. To make a waist casing for the elastic, turn the top edge of the skirt down ⅜ inch (9.5 mm), and press. Turn under again ⅝ inch (1.6 cm), and press again. Stitch the edge of the casing, leaving a 1-inch (2.5 cm) opening for threading the elastic.

11. Cut the elastic to the waist measurement plus 1 inch (2.5 cm) for overlapping the ends. Attach a safety pin to one end of the elastic, and thread it through the casing. Note: Be careful to avoid twisting the elastic in the casing. Overlap the ends, and stitch them together. Stitch the opening closed. Press the skirt.

12. To make a waist casing for the drawstring ribbon, fold the skirt in half to find the center seam. Press under the top raw edge of the skirt ¼ inch (6 mm), then press under again 1 inch (2.5 cm). On the front, draw two vertical lines for buttonholes, each positioned ¼ inch (6 mm) from the center seam. Draw each buttonhole line ⅝ inch (1.6 cm) long.

13. Open up the casing and fuse a small piece of fusible interfacing behind both buttonhole lines. Make both buttonholes. Cut a length of ribbon to measure the waist of the skirt plus 12 inches (30.5 cm).

14. Refold the raw edges at your earlier ¼ inch (6 mm) and 1 inch (2.5 cm) lines. Pin the casing down and topstitch close to the edge from the wrong side of the fabric. Feed the ribbon through the casing, in one buttonhole and out the other. Gather to fit and tie with a bow.

Charity

Children of the Forest
www.childrenoftheforest.com

Children of the Forest is a nonprofit in Thailand that provides schools and homes for Karen, Mon, and Burmese refugee children near the Thai-Burmese border. In this area, where refugees face a life entrenched in poverty, the Karen and Mon people have been subjected to much suffering. The organization's mission is to address the refugees' grievances, ease their suffering, and restore their dignity. The nonprofit runs eight schools with a total of 500 students, most of whom are studying for the first time in their lives. Focusing on the critical issues of education, health care, and children in distress, Children of the Forest strives to remove obstacles to happiness and create routes to hope and opportunity.

OTHER APPROPRIATE CHARITIES FOR THE SKIRT:

Youth Action International (page 49)

ORPHANetwork (page 31)

Pan de Vida (page 17)

Designer: *Jenny B Harris*

Pupkins

This playful pair of pups will capture the hearts of children around the world. Follow the instructions to make one dog, then dress the pup in overalls or a dress.

Basic Sewing Kit (page 124)

Templates (pages 134 and 135)

Scrap of print cotton fabric, no smaller than 5 x 6 inches (12.7 x 15.2 cm), for the inner ears

Scrap of fusible interfacing, no smaller than 5 x 6 inches (12.7 x 15.2 cm)

White felt, 12 x 16 inches (30.5 x 40.6 cm), for the body

Light blue felt, 3 x 4 inches (7.6 x 10.2 cm), for the muzzle

Black felt scrap for the eyes and nose

Red felt, 5 x 6 inches (12.7 x 15.2 cm), for the mouth and shoes

Print cotton fabric, 12 x 14 inches (30.5 x 35.6 cm), for the boy's overalls

Print cotton fabric, 8 x 16 inches (20.3 x 40.6 cm), for the girl's dress

Contrasting print cotton fabric, 4 x 8 inches (10.2 x 20.3 cm), for the dress waistband

Water-soluble fabric marker

White embroidery floss

All-purpose thread in light blue, black, red, and white

Knitting needle

Polyester fiberfill

1 inch (2.5 cm) of hook-and-loop tape, ½ inch (1.3 cm) wide

Charity

Alex's Lemonade Stand
www.alexslemonade.org

Alex's Lemonade Stand was founded by four-year-old cancer patient Alex Scott (1996–2004). Her simple concept was to sell lemonade to raise money to cure cancer. Alex's spirited determination to raise awareness and money for childhood cancer while she bravely fought her own terminal illness has inspired thousands of people from all walks of life to raise money and give to her cause. These stuffed puppies will bring a lot of love to children recovering from cancer treatment, and the organization also plans to give them to the siblings of children undergoing treatment.

OTHER APPROPRIATE CHARITIES FOR THE PUPKINS:

Project Night Night (page 21)
Giving Children Hope (page 69)
Pediatric unit of your local hospital

MAKE THE PUPKIN

1. Copy and enlarge the templates on pages 134 and 135, and cut the pieces out. Note: Pay attention to the placement markings on the templates. When you cut the fabric pieces, you will need to transfer the lines to the fabric using the water-soluble fabric marker.

2. Make the ears: Follow the manufacturer's instructions to apply the fusible interfacing to the wrong side of the print cotton fabric for the inner ears. Trace and then cut two ear pieces from the fabric. Make sure you flip the pattern piece before tracing the second ear. Then cut two ears from the white felt. Lay an inner ear right side up over a felt ear. Use the white embroidery floss to blanket stitch around the edges. Repeat for the other ear. Note: You do not stuff the ears.

Hope Note

I hope that the children will be enveloped in the love and care that has been poured into every one of the gifts sent. I hope they'll know the love from around the world that's being sent to them in the most tangible of ways.

Annwen, Canada

3. Make the face: Cut the two head/torso pieces from the felt. Using the water-soluble marker, transfer all the placement lines to the front of one piece of felt. Using the placement lines as your guide, lay the muzzle on the face. With the light blue thread, whipstitch around the edge of the muzzle. Position the eyes and nose, and whipstitch in place using the black all-purpose thread. Position the mouth, and whipstitch securely in place using the red all-purpose thread.

4. Sew the head/torso together: Lay the front right side up on top of the back piece. Using the transferred placement lines as a guide, slip the ears, fabric side up, in between the front and back pieces. Start sewing at point A. Use the whipstitch to sew up one side, around the head, and down the other side, ending at point B. Leave the bottom edge open. Before stuffing, smooth the seams by running the point of the knitting needle along the stitches; this will shift the edges of the felt so they butt together.

5. Stuff the head/torso using the polyester fiberfill. Make sure to evenly stuff all the way around the head. Do not pack the stuffing too tightly, but make sure it's firm enough for the head to stay upright. Once stuffed, whipstitch the bottom opening to close it.

6. Cut the arms, legs, and tail pieces from white felt. Whipstitch the side seams of the arms, legs, and tail with the white all-purpose thread. Leave the ends open for stuffing. Stuff the pieces, being careful to not stuff too tightly.

7. Pinch the tops of the legs flat with seams to the side, and whipstitch them closed. Do the same for the base of the tail. Pinch the tops of the arms flat with the seams together, and whipstitch them closed. Make sure you've marked the angle for the arm placement on both sides of the torso. Pin the arms to the torso along this angle with seams aligned. Whipstitch the arms into place.

8. Stitch the legs to the bottom of the torso, making sure the legs can fold forward into a sitting position. Stitch the tail to the back of the torso.

BOY'S OVERALLS

1. Use the templates on page 135 to cut the overalls, facing, and straps. Cut the pocket from red felt.

2. Make the straps: Fold and press the long edge of one strap in ⅛ inch (3 mm). Repeat on the other long edge. Then fold the strap in half, and top stitch it ⅛ inch (3 mm) in from the edge. Repeat for the other strap.

3. Whipstitch the pocket onto the overall piece using red thread, leaving the top edge open like a pocket. Hem the bottom edge of the overalls. Fold under ¼ inch (6 mm), and press. Fold under again and press, then topstitch the hem in place.

4. Lay the overall piece right side up. Position the straps on the placement lines, and pin in place with raw edges aligned. Lay the facing right side down over the overalls and straps. Align the edges, and pin in place. Use a ¼-inch (6 mm) seam allowance to stitch the edge from point D to E. Clip the corners and curves. Turn and press.

5. Put the overall on the Pupkin, position the straps inside the back edge, and pin in place. Remove the overall from the doll, and topstitch ⅛ inch (3 mm) in from the edge from point F to G to secure the straps.

6. Turn the overall inside out. Fold the side seams in to the center, slightly overlapping the mid-point, and pin the front to the back. Stitch a V through both layers to form the crotch. Cut the center of the V, ending close to the line for the top of the crotch. Trim close to the stitching line (figure 1).

7. Turn the overall right side out, and press. Sew the hook-and-loop tape to the back and flap of the overall for the closure.

FIGURE 1

GIRL'S DRESS

1. Use the templates on pages 134 and 135 to cut the dress skirt and two straps from one fabric, and the waistband and waistband facing from the contrasting fabric.

2. Make the straps: Fold and press the long edge of one strap in ⅛ inch (3 mm). Repeat on the other long edge. Then fold the strap in half, and topstitch it ⅛ inch (3 mm) in from the edge. Repeat for the other strap.

3. Hem the sides of the skirt: Fold under ¼ inch (6 mm), and press. Fold under again and press, then topstitch the hem in place. Do the same along the bottom edge of the skirt.

4. Sew a gathering stitch along the top edge of the skirt, approximately ¼ inch (6 mm) from the edge. Pull the thread, then evenly space the gathers on the waistband between points F and G with right sides together. Pin in place. Stitch slightly below the gather line, then press with the gathered edge up.

5. Fold the bottom edge of the waistband facing under ¼ inch (6 mm), press, and sew. Clip at the marks.

6. Lay the skirt right side up. Position the straps on the placement lines and pin in place with raw edges aligned.

7. Lay the waistband facing right side down over the waistband and straps. Align the edges, and pin in place. Use a ¼-inch (6 mm) seam allowance to stitch the edge from point H to J. Clip the corners, turn, and press. Note: If desired, you can hand sew the waistband facing to the back of the skirt.

8. Put the dress around the Pupkin, position the straps inside the back edge, and pin in place. Remove the dress from the doll. Topstitch ⅛ inch (3 mm) in from the edge (from point H to J) to secure the straps.

9. Bring the sides of the skirt together, overlapping them ¼ inch (6 mm). Stitch up from the bottom hem of the skirt, stopping approximately 1 inch (2.5 cm) from the top to leave room for the tail. Sew hook-and-loop tape to the back of the waistband for the closure.

SHOES

1. Use the pattern to cut the shoes from the felt as indicated.

2. With red thread, stitch the shoes together using a tiny whipstitch. Smooth the seams by running a knitting needle along the stitches.

3. Use white embroidery floss to embroider laces on the fronts of the boy's sneakers.

Necklace & Earrings

Everyone deserves to shine on her special night. Add some sparkle to a young woman's prom with this easy-to-bead necklace and earring set that can be donated to an organization that provides girls with gowns and accessories.

Designer: *Beth Sweet*

Hope Note

Thank you so much for giving me the chance to feel like a princess. Not only was I worried about not being able to go to my prom, I was also worried about my mom because she had been sick. Prom just wasn't in the cards for us, and if it weren't for your organization, I wouldn't have been able to go. On the big night, I could see the tears welling up in my parents' eyes, and I felt like I had given them the same gift you had given me. For the first time in a long time my mom was truly happy. I would love to donate my dress to Cinderella's Closet so I can give back what I experienced last year. My mom and I both filled out the registry to volunteer this year and we can't wait.

Alexandra, Kentucky

Necklace & Earrings

Crimping pliers

Round-nose pliers

Chain-nose pliers

Materials for Necklace

22-inch (55.9 cm) length of beading wire, 0.012 inch (0.3 mm) in diameter

4 crimp beads

Lobster claw clasp

Approximately 110 white seed beads, size 6

8 gold cubic seed beads, size 6

4 fire-polished crystal beads, 4 mm

2 gold fire-polished crystal beads, 12 mm

8 fire-polished crystal beads, 6 mm

7 white shell beads

Materials for Earrings

2 ear wires

2 silver chandelier 5-drop earring findings

10 headpins (5 for each earring), each 2 inches (5.1 cm)

10 gold crystal beads, each 6 mm

10 gold cubic seed beads, size 6

10 white seed beads, size 6

30 fire-polished crystal beads, each 4 mm

Finished Size

Necklace: 17 inches (43.2 cm)

Earrings: each 2¾ inches (7 cm)

NOTE This necklace is designed to be simple and versatile: it consists of a sequence of focal beads strung between two segments of seed beads. The first segment is 5 inches (12.7 cm) of seed beads; the central segment is 7 inches (17.8 cm) of focal beads; and the last segment is another 5 inches (12.7 cm) of seed beads. This design has a very different look when it's created with deep-toned colors and natural textures, as pictured below.

NECKLACE

1. Slide one end of the beading wire through two crimp beads, through the hole of the first piece of the clasp, and then back through the crimp beads, so about 1 inch (2.5 cm) of wire has passed through. Using the crimping pliers, close both crimps.

2. String one gold cubic seed bead followed by the first 5-inch (12.7 cm) segment of white seed beads. Allow beads to cover the 1-inch (2.5 cm) tail of wire.

3. String the 7-inch (17.8 cm) central segment of focal beads as follows:

1 cubic gold seed bead, size 6
2 fire-polished crystal beads, size 6
1 cubic gold seed bead, size 6
1 gold fire-polished crystal bead, 12 mm
1 cubic gold seed bead, size 6
8 fire-polished crystal beads, 6mm, alternating with 7 white shell beads
1 cubic gold seed bead, size 6
1 gold fire-polished crystal bead, 12 mm
1 cubic gold seed bead, size 6
2 fire-polished crystal beads, size 6
1 cubic gold seed bead, size 6

4. String the last 5-inch (12.7 cm) segment of white seed beads and the last gold cubic seed bead.

5. Slide the end of the wire through two crimp beads, through the hole of the second piece of the clasp, and then back through the crimp beads and 1 inch (2.5 cm) of seed beads. Using the crimping pliers, close both crimps. Trim the excess wire.

EARRINGS

1. Each earring consists of one ear wire, one silver chandelier 5-drop earring finding, and five 2-inch (5.1 cm) headpins. String the following beads onto each headpin:

1 fire-polished gold crystal bead, 6mm
1 cubic gold seed bead, size 6
1 white seed bead, size 6
3 fire-polished crystal beads, 4 mm

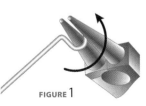

FIGURE 1

2. Using the chain-nose pliers, bend the end of a head-pin 90° and trim the wire so that ⅜ inch (.95 cm) remains. Using the round-nose pliers, make a simple loop by grasping the wire end and rolling the pliers until the wire touches the 90° bend (figure 1). Repeat for the other four headpins.

3. Attach the five headpins to the 5-drop finding, and attach the finding to an ear wire. Repeat for the second earring.

Charity

Cinderella's Closet of Northern Kentucky
www.cinderellasclosetnky.org

Cinderella's Closet of Northern Kentucky began when its founder overheard a teenager at a consignment store ask her foster mother if they could afford a gently used gown for her prom. Hearing the $35 price was out of the family's reach, Erin Peterson bought the dress for the girl, who thanked her tearfully, saying she would look "just like Cinderella" in the gown. The organization now has three locations, and—with the assistance of many volunteer "Fairy Godmothers"—helps almost 1,000 girls who otherwise could not afford it find dresses, shoes, and accessories for their schools' formals and proms. The organization believes it's important to not just give gowns to girls, but to do so in a way that helps the girls feel loved and special.

OTHER APPROPRIATE CHARITIES FOR THE EARRINGS AND NECKLACE:

Local charities that donate prom dresses and accessories

SafePlace (page 117)

New Orleans Women's Shelter (page 67)

Designer: *Lisa Cox*

Care Caps

This warm, soft beanie will be appreciated by anyone who experiences hair loss during chemotherapy or radiation. The secret heart sewn into the beanie's lining shows that it was made with love.

Basic Sewing Kit (page 124)

Hat template (page 131)

Heart template (page 131)

¼ yard (22.9 cm) of polar fleece for small; ⅜ yard (34.3 cm) each for medium or large

¼ yard (22.9 cm) of flannel for small; ⅜ yard (34.3 cm) each for medium or large

Scrap of red cotton fabric, approximately 2 inches (5 cm) square

Paper-backed fusible web

1 large and 1 small button

Seam Allowance
½ inch (1.3 cm), unless otherwise noted

Sizing
Small (child's) to fit a head circumference of 20 to 22 inches (50.8 to 55.9 cm)
Medium (ladies') to fit a head circumference of 21 to 24 inches (53.3 to 61 cm)
Large (men's) to fit a head circumference of 22 to 25 inches (55.9 to 63.5 cm)

---

1. Copy and enlarge the hat template on page 131. Cut out the fabrics. You will need four pieces each from the fleece and flannel lining.

2. Cut one strip from the fleece for the hatband: The width and length of the band is determined by the size of hat you're making. For a small hat, cut a strip 8 x 22 inches (20.3 x 55.9 cm). For a medium hat, cut a strip 8½ x 24 inches (21.6 x 61 cm). For a large hat, cut a strip 8½ x 26 inches (21.6 x 66 cm).

Charity

MD Anderson Cancer Center
www.mdanderson.org

The University of Texas MD Anderson Cancer Center's mission is to eliminate cancer in Texas, the nation, and the world through outstanding programs that integrate patient care, research, and prevention—and through education for undergraduate and graduate students, trainees, professionals, employees, and the public. The full mailing address is available on the website; please add Department of Volunteer Services, Unit 115, when mailing care caps for patients.

OTHER APPROPRIATE CHARITIES FOR THE CARE CAPS:

Local cancer treatment hospitals

Local homeless shelters

LOWO Child and Family Services (page 77)

Hope Note

Participating in Craft Hope has given me the opportunity to give love to people of the world who I would not be able to reach otherwise, people who are so worthy of love.

Anna, Alaska

3. Copy the heart shape on page 131, and cut it out. Trace the heart shape onto the paper side of the fusible web. Cut around the shape, leaving a 2½-inch (6.4 cm) border. Follow the manufacturer's instructions to adhere the fusible web to the red fabric. Cut out the heart. Remove the paper backing. Center the shape on the right side of one of the lining pieces, and press to affix. Sew around the edges of the heart to finish, using a buttonhole or zigzag stitch.

4. Sew the flannel lining: Place two lining pieces together with the right sides facing, and sew from the crown to the brim. Clip the seams, and press open. Repeat, using the remaining two pieces of lining. Place the two lining units together with the right sides facing, and sew from one side to the other. Clip the seams, and press them open.

5. Sew the fleece: Place two fleece pieces together with the right sides facing. Sew from the crown to the brim. Clip the seams, and press open. On the right side, topstitch ¼ inch (6 mm) from both sides of the seam. Repeat, using the remaining two pieces of fleece. Place the two fleece units together with the right sides facing, and sew from one side to to the other. Clip the seams, and press them open. Topstitch ¼ inch (6 mm) from both sides of the seam.

6. Slip the lining inside the fleece with wrong sides together, matching up the crown and side seams, and pin. If you've used a thick fleece, you might find that the lining is too long. If so, trim the lining approximately ⅛ to ¼ inch (3 to 6 mm) around the circumference of the cap until it's flush with the fleece.

7. With the right sides facing to form a circle, sew the short ends of the hatband together. Fold the band in half lengthwise with wrong sides facing. Divide the band into quarters, marking each point with a pin.

TIP When working with several thicknesses of fabric, particularly fluffy fleece, it's easy to miss a stitch or two when seaming. Make sure the hatband is firmly attached before finishing the raw edge in step 8.

8. Pin the band to the cap with right sides facing. Align all raw edges. Match the pins used to mark the quadrants with the seams. You may have to stretch the band slightly to fit the circumference of the hat. Stitch the layers together using a ¼-inch (6 mm) seam allowance. Finish the raw edge with a zigzag or overlock stitch.

9. Lay the small button on top of the large button, and sew them as one securely to the hatband.

Designer: *Susan Wasinger*

Seed Balls

Seed balls—tidy packets of seeds mixed with dense, fertile compost and wrapped in protective jackets of mineral-rich clay— can bring fallow soil to life. The clay in each ball keeps the seeds from being blown away or eaten by a bird. Once rain melts the clay, the seeds germinate in their own tiny patch of compost.

Seeds for flowers, herbs, grasses, or ground cover (see note below)

Good quality compost

Container for mixing

Powdered clay

Water

Newspaper

Charity
A local organization

Because of the danger of invasive species, this project needs to be donated locally with extra care taken to be sure all the seeds used are native and noninvasive. Contact a local organization that builds houses for the homeless, a neighborhood revitalization group, or a nearby community garden collective to donate your seed balls. Seeds also make a thoughtful gift of hope for anyone going through a difficult time.

NOTE: It's essential to use only the seeds of plant species native to your area. To start an instant, thriving ecosystem, use seeds from a variety of native species, and try to include at least one nitrogen-fixing plant (such as soybeans, clover, or alfalfa) in the mix.

1. Combine two parts mixed seeds with three parts compost in a container. Stir in five parts powdered red or brown clay. Moisten with water, and mix with your hands until pliable.

   TIP Red and brown clays are richer in the minerals that help your seedlings get a good start. Powdered clays are a mainstay of ceramists, so check with local potters for a source. Powdered red clay is also used by the beauty industry for skin care and is often available in smaller quantities.

2. Now you're ready to roll. Pinch off a penny-sized hunk of the clay mixture, and roll it between the palms of your hands until it forms into a tight ball. The sphere should be about ¾ inch (1.9 cm) in diameter. Do the same with all of the clay mixture. Set the balls on a newspaper, and allow them to dry for 24 to 48 hours; then store them in a cool, dry place until ready to sow.

3. Lay out the seed balls in late winter or early spring at a density of about 10 or more per square yard (.83 m²). They will germinate when the time is right.

Designer: *Dana Willard*

Burp Cloths & Crib Sheets

Caretakers everywhere will confirm that cotton burp cloths are a necessity. And because the cribs in orphanages are often small, standard or king-sized pillowcases are the perfect size to serve as sheets.

Basic Sewing Kit (page 124)

1½ yards (1.3 m) of white cotton muslin or fashion gauze for the burp cloths

⅞ yard (80 cm) of white cotton flannel for the burp cloths

Cotton fabric scraps or recycled T-shirts for the appliqués

1 standard or king-size pillowcase, or 1 yard (.9 m) of white woven cotton sheeting for the sheet

Cardstock

All-purpose thread in various colors

Fray retardant (optional)

NOTE: All fabric is 44 inches (111.8 cm) wide.

BURP CLOTHS

1. Wash and dry the white muslin or gauze and the white flannel. If extremely wrinkled, iron the muslin before cutting.

2. Use the cardstock to make a rectangular pattern that is 10 x 14 inches (25.4 x 35.6 cm). Note: Burp cloths can be any size. However, to maximize your yardage, this size rectangle works well and will yield six burp cloths from the 1½ yards (1.3 m) of fabric.

3. Fold the white muslin or gauze in half selvage to selvage. Turn the fabric with the fold at the bottom and the selvages at the top. Align the pattern to the left side of the fabric with the rectangle's longer side on the fold. Trace around the pattern. Move the pattern on the fabric to trace five more rectangles. Cut out the rectangles. You should have a total of 12 rectangles.

4. Following the same process as in step 3, trace three rectangles on the white flannel, and cut them out. You will trace the rectangle three times and cut a total of six rectangles.

Charity

ORPHANetwork
www.orphanetwork.org

La Chureca is the city garbage dump in Managua, Nicaragua. Approximately 1,500 people, many of them children, live in and survive off the trash there, scavenging for anything of value. It's difficult to put words to the devastation that these families experience each day living amongst the smoldering piles of trash. One of the most difficult sights is that of a small child, often barely clothed, searching through the garbage for a scrap of recyclable materials or something to eat. Tucked away in a neighborhood right outside of La Chureca is Verbo's El Fado church. A small, rented building with a few rooms and a kitchen, this church aims to bring hope to the families of La Chureca. One of their services is a free day care center that is open every weekday to allow the women in La Chureca to bring their young children to receive care, attention, and a daily meal while the mothers work in the landfill. ORPHANetwork has asked for burp cloths and crib sheets to help with the efforts.

OTHER APPROPRIATE CHARITIES FOR THE BURP CLOTHS & CRIB SHEETS:

Giving Children Hope (page 69)

Children of the Forest (page 93)

Most orphanages

Hope Note

What a wonderful way to teach my little ones about the blessings they have, and how we can share our love with others.

Chris, Idaho

5. Each burp cloth has a flannel layer between two muslin or gauze pieces to provide extra absorbency. Place one muslin or gauze rectangle right side down on your work surface. Place one flannel rectangle on it. Lay one muslin or gauze rectangle right side up on the two layers. Align the edges, and pin the layers together along the edges.

6. Choose a design or motif for your appliqués. Simple shapes such as a heart, star, sunshine, tree, moon, apple, bird, butterfly, flower, or leaves, are easiest to work with. Draw or transfer your designs onto the cardstock, and cut them out to make your patterns. Note: You might to look online for simple shapes you can print and then transfer to your cardstock.

7. Select the fabric scraps you want to use for the appliqués. Knits work well because they're soft and provide extra absorbency. You can use woven cottons, but the edges may fray over time. Trace the shapes onto the fabric scraps, and cut them out.

8. Position your appliqués on the layers you pinned together in step 5, pin in place, and sew. Use a white bobbin and a top thread color that contrasts with the color of your appliqué. Stitch around each appliqué, sewing ⅛ inch (3 mm) in from the edges.

> **TIP** When sewing appliqués made of knit fabric, use a ballpoint needle, and avoid tugging or pulling the fabric through the needle as you sew because it will stretch the appliqués. Go slowly when you stitch around curves. You may need to lift your presser foot now and again to smooth out the fabric.

9. Using a ⅜-inch (9.5 mm) seam allowance, stitch around the raw edges of the burp cloth. Then, using a serger or a tight zigzag or overcast stitch on your sewing machine, finish the raw edges. For an extra pop of color, use a bright contrasting color of thread to finish the edges.

10. Trim the threads. If desired, place a small drop of fray retardant on each corner of the cloth to decrease fraying.

CRIB SHEET

1. Wash and iron a standard or king-size pillowcase (new or recycled). If you're making your sheet from the cotton sheeting, cut two rectangles, each approximately 20 x 30 inches (50.8 x 76.2 cm).

2. If you are using a pillowcase, pin around the edges through both layers, but do not cut along the edges. If you are using fabric, place the rectangles together, wrong sides facing, and pin around the edges through both layers. For either the pillowcase or fabric, use white thread to sew around the edges, using a ½-inch (1.3 cm) seam allowance.

3. As you did in steps 6, 7, and 8 for the burp cloths, cut and sew the appliqués to the sheet. Use a white bobbin and a top thread color that contrasts with the color of your appliqué.

4. Finish the edge of the sheet: If you made the sheet from a pillowcase, use a wide zigzag stitch to sew around the edges. If you made the sheet from fabric, use a serger (or a tight zigzag or overcast stitch on your sewing machine) to sew around the edges. To add some spice to the edges, use a white bobbin, and thread the top of the machine with a bright contrasting color.

Hope Note

The blanket and handkerchiefs have been made with love, and I hope that love will be felt by the babies who will receive the items.

Muriel, The Netherlands

Designer: *Wendi Gratz*

Dog Tug Toy

Humane societies and animal rescue centers rely on contributions for a variety of needs—everything from bedding and food to human companionship. Donate this rugged, easy-to-macramé tug toy, and you'll make tails wag at your favorite shelter.

12 yards (11 m) of 6 mm macramé cord

Lighter or matches

Duct tape

Awl or paring knife

2 mini tennis balls, each 2 inches (5 cm) in diameter

Large-eye upholstery needle at least 2 inches (5 cm) long

Pliers

Finished size: 2½ x 28½ inches (6.4 x 72.4 cm)

Charity

Local Animal Shelter or Rescue Group

Experts estimate the United States has somewhere between 12 and 15 million stray and abandoned animals. Each year, 6 to 8 million of these animals enter animal shelters. Local rescue groups and shelters provide these animals with food, shelter, and care, and sometimes reunite them with their owners or find them a new family. Most animal shelters and rescue groups struggle financially, and so donations of money, food, bedding, and pet toys are almost always welcome. Better yet, macramé the tug toy, and volunteer your time to walk, groom, or play with the dogs at your local shelter.

1. Cut two lengths of macramé cord, each 3 feet (91.4 cm) long. Cut two lengths of cord, each 15 feet (4.5 m) long. Prevent the ends from fraying by melting them with the lighter. Work in a well-ventilated area, and make sure to protect your hands from the melting plastic.

2. Gather all four cords, and use an overhand knot to tie them together at one end.

3. Tape the knotted end of the cords to your work surface to hold it in place. Position the cords with the two short ones in the middle and the two long ones pulled out to the left and right.

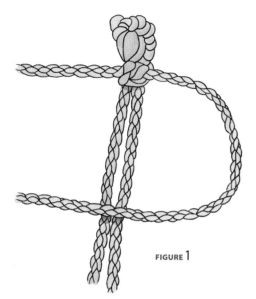

FIGURE 1

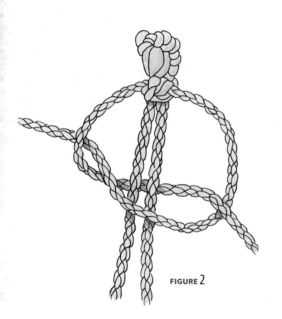

FIGURE 2

4. Macramé a twist stitch. (If you've never macraméd, don't worry: This is a really simple repeating stitch.) Start by placing the right cord over the two center cords (figure 1). Run the left cord over and then under the tail of the right cord, then under the two center cords, and finally over the loop created by the right cord (figure 2). Pull the tails as tight as you can. Repeat until you have 8 inches (20.3 cm) of twist.

5. Using the awl or paring knife, poke a hole in opposite sides of a mini tennis ball. You just made a bead! Make another bead using the second tennis ball.

6. Using the needle, thread the center cords through the holes in one of the tennis balls. The rubber in the balls tends to grab whatever you're threading, so you may need to use the pliers to pull the needle and thread through. You may also find it easier to thread one cord at a time. Pull the tennis ball snug to the twist.

7. Repeat step 4 until you have another 6 inches (15.2 cm) of twist after the ball. Pretend as if the tennis ball isn't even there when making the first knot after threading the ball—the cords will simply frame each side.

8. Thread on the second tennis ball, and repeat step 4 until you've made another 8 inches (20.3 cm) of twist.

9. Tie the ends using an overhand knot, trim, and melt the cut ends to seal. The macramé is durable enough for unsupervised chewing.

Flowered Purse

These days, women reentering the job market need to build a suitable wardrobe. Providing the boost of confidence that can seal the deal in a job interview, this stylish handbag is perfect for a woman returning to work or starting a new life.

Designer: **Rebeka Lambert**

Flowered Purse

Hope Note

It's nice to be a part of something bigger than myself.

Mary Ellen, New Jersey

Basic Sewing Kit (page 124)

Template (page 129)

½ yard (45.7 cm) of red floral print fabric for the exterior

½ yard (45.7 cm) of brown floral print fabric for the lining

½ yard (45.7 cm) of fusible fleece

½ yard (45.7 cm) of heavyweight fusible interfacing

Water-soluble fabric marker

Thread, coordinating color

Magnetic snap

Seam Allowance
½ inch (1.3 cm), unless otherwise noted

What You Cut

Red Floral Print
1 piece, 4½ x 21 inches (11.4 x 53.3 cm), for the strap

Lining
2 pieces, each 5 x 10 inches (12.7 x 25.4 cm), for the pocket

Heavyweight Interfacing
1 piece, 5 x 10 inches (12.7 x 25.4 cm), for the pocket
1 piece, 4½ x 21 inches (11.4 x 53.3 cm), for the strap

1. Copy and enlarge the template on page 129, and cut it out. Cut all pieces as indicated for the exterior and lining. Cut a front and back from the fusible fleece to interface the exterior of the bag. Cut a front and back from the heavyweight interfacing for the lining. Follow the cutting guide to cut the fabrics for the pocket and strap.

2. Follow the manufacturer's instructions to adhere the fusible fleece to the wrong side of each of the exterior pieces. Then follow the manufacturer's instructions to adhere the heavyweight fusible interfacing to the wrong side of each lining piece, each pocket piece, and the strap.

3. Use the water-soluble fabric marker to transfer the placement of the darts onto the wrong side of the fabric at the bottom corners. Do this on both the exterior fabric and the lining. Sew the darts. Fold the fabric wrong side out along the center of each dart. Sew on the marked lines, backstitching at the point of each dart to secure the stitching.

4. Make the pocket by pinning the two pocket pieces with right sides together. Starting on one short side, sew around the edges, leaving a 2- to 3-inch (5 to 7.6 cm) opening for turning. Clip the corners, and turn the pocket. Fold and press the edges of the opening into the seam allowance. Position the pocket on one side of the lining and pin. Stitch close to the edge of the pocket along its sides and bottom.

5. Make the strap by first folding it in half lengthwise with wrong sides together. Press the fold. Open the strap, then fold each of the long sides into the center fold, and press. Refold the strap in half along the center fold, and press. Edge stitch around all four edges of the strap.

6. Follow the manufacturer's instructions for attaching one half of the magnetic snap to the flap of the lining. Position it at the center of the flap, 1½ inches (3.8 cm) in from the rounded edge. Attach the other half of the magnetic snap to the exterior front, positioning it at the center of the purse and 3 inches (7.6 cm) down from the top edge.

7. Pin the exterior front and back together with right sides facing. Sew the sides and bottom. Repeat for the purse lining.

8. Pin the purse strap to each side of the purse exterior, centering the strap on the side seams and aligning the raw edges.

9. With the exterior turned right side out, insert it into the lining that is wrong side out. The right sides of both the exterior and lining should be facing, with the strap sandwiched in between. Align the raw edges, and pin through both layers around the flap and front of the purse.

10. Start sewing along the front of the purse. When you get to the side seam, lift the presser foot and pivot the fabric on the needle. Sew along the flap, pivot on the other side seam, and sew back across the front. Stop sewing a few inches from where you started, in order to leave an opening for turning.

11. Clip into the seam allowance at the pivot points so the corners will be sharp when turned. Be careful to avoid cutting the stitches. Trim the excess fabric around the flap to reduce bulk.

12. Turn the bag right side out. Gently tug on the straps to make sure that everything is fully turned. If needed, use a knitting needle to push out the corners. Stuff the lining inside the bag, then press the purse to smooth everything out. Fold and press the edges of the opening into the seam allowance. Topstitch around the entire top edge of the bag, using a ¼-inch (6 mm) seam allowance.

Charity

SafePlace
www.safeplace.org

SafePlace, located in Austin, Texas, seeks to end sexual and domestic violence through safety, healing, prevention, and social change. The organization offers such services as a 24-hour hotline; accompaniment for survivors of rape in need of support for forensic and physical medical examinations; an emergency shelter for women and children escaping domestic violence; an off-site shelter for men seeking safety; sliding-scale legal assistance for survivors of rape, sexual abuse, or domestic violence; and a transitional services program that helps women rebuild their lives free of family violence; and counseling and educational programs for the prevention of dating violence, sexual assault/abuse, domestic violence, and bullying.

OTHER APPROPRIATE CHARITIES FOR THE PURSE:

Organizations that help women returning to work

Local women's shelters

Local foster care programs for teens

Designer: *Cathie Fillian*

Tie-Dyed Snapsuit

All moms know how useful this elemental piece of clothing can be, and every baby deserves one that's been created with love. This project features easy dyeing and embroidery techniques—little extras that give the suit a customized feel.

Basic sewing kit (page 124)

Bird template (page 133)

Snapsuit, 100% cotton

Turquoise fabric dye

Large glass or plastic bowl

Baby clothes hanger

Fine-line embroidery marker

Embroidery hoop

Ballpoint embroidery needle

Embroidery floss in turquoise, lime, and black

Seam Allowance
¼ inch (1.3 cm), unless otherwise noted

1. Prewash the snapsuit to remove any sizing. Copy the bird template on page 133.

2. Prepare the dye in the large bowl following the manufacturer's instructions. Thoroughly wet the snapsuit, and hang it on the baby hanger. Hold the snapsuit over the dye bath, and then slowly lower it in, dyeing only the bottom section. Keep the fabric in the dye for a few minutes. Remove it from the dye bath, and rinse it until the water runs clear. Hang to dry.

3. Place the bird template in between the layers of the snapsuit, and move it into the desired position on the front. Use the fine-line embroidery marker to trace it onto the fabric.

> **TIP** When you use a water-soluble embroidery marker, you can simply eliminate any stray lines by washing the snapsuit. If you use an air-soluble marker, the lines will magically disappear in 12 to 24 hours without washing.

4. Place the front of the snapsuit into the embroidery hoop. Using the ballpoint embroidery needle and four strands of the turquoise floss, embroider the outer edges of the bird using a running stitch. Using four strands of lime floss, embroider the leaf stem using the running stitch and the leaf using a satin stitch. Use two strands of black floss to embroider the tip of the beak and the eye of the bird.

Charity

MotherLove Program
www.ywcaofasheville.org

The MotherLove Program at the YWCA of Asheville, North Carolina, matches adult mentors with pregnant and parenting teens. Mentors provide needed support, guidance, and friendship while teaching parenting skills to these young mothers. In addition, the program provides Adolescent Pregnancy Prevention educational sessions and one-on-one counseling on pregnancy programs throughout the community. The MotherLove program believes that every teen mother has a purpose and a destiny. It tries to instill the teens with an understanding that they are strong women who can overcome any obstacle in their lives—such as being a teenage mom while staying in high school and then going on to college.

OTHER APPROPRIATE CHARITIES FOR THE SNAPSUIT:

Miracle Foundation (page 73)

LOWO Child and Family Services (page 77)

Giving Children Hope (page 69)

Local programs for teen mothers

Designer: *Ellie Beck*

Stenciled Book Bag

Book totes are great gifts for both children and adults, especially those learning to read or studying a new language. Consider tucking a few books into this bag before giving it away.

Basic Sewing Kit (page 124)

1 yard (.9 m) of plain woven cotton, linen, or hemp, for the outside of the bag

1 yard (.9 m) of cotton fabric, either plain or print, for the lining

Iron-on interfacing (optional)

Stencil designs (page 128)

Tracing paper

Self-adhesive shelf paper

Craft knife and cutting mat

Fabric stencil paint in black, brown, blue, and green

Stencil Brush

Thread

What You Cut

Woven Fabric
2 pieces, each 18 x 25 inches (45.7 x 63.5 cm)
2 strips, each 2 x 22 inches (5 x 55.9 cm), for the straps

Lining
2 pieces, each 18 x 25 inches (45.7 x 63.5 cm)
2 strips, each 2 x 22 inches (5 x 55.9 cm), for the straps

Interfacing (optional)
2 pieces, each 2 x 22 inches (5 x 55.9 cm), for the straps

STENCIL THE FABRIC

1. Trace the design on page 128, and transfer it onto two pieces of the self-adhesive shelf paper to make two stencils. On one piece, transfer only the tree trunk. On the other piece, transfer only the leaves.

2. Place the paper on the cutting mat, and use the craft knife to carefully cut out the motifs from each of the stencils. Note: Use a smooth cutting motion to avoid making jagged edges.

3. Center the stencil with the tree trunk onto the right side of one of the outside pieces. Carefully remove the paper backing from the shelf paper while smoothing the stencil on the fabric with a steady pressure to ease out any air bubbles.

Charity

Literacy Volunteers of Atlanta
www.lvama.org

The mission of Literacy Volunteers of Atlanta is to increase adult and family literacy, primarily through volunteer tutoring. LVA brings volunteer tutors and students together on a one-on-one basis with instruction geared to the needs of the individual student. The student-centered, whole-language method focuses on reading for meaning, comprehension, and real-life applications. Students set their own goals; the staff at LVA assists the students with defining these goals. LVA's objective is to empower students to become functionally literate, contributing members of society. It features four main programs: Adult Basic Literacy, English for Speakers of Other Languages (ESOL), Family Literacy, and Workplace Literacy.

OTHER APPROPRIATE CHARITIES FOR THE STENCILED BOOK BAG:

Books for Kids
(www.booksforkids.org.au)

Hearts in Unity (page 13)

Local literacy programs

Hope Note

A great cause! Count me in!

Linda, Malaysia

4. Use the stencil brush to apply the black or brown fabric paint. Don't work with back-and-forth brush strokes; instead, hold the brush upright, and move it up and down to dab the paint onto the fabric—this is called stippling. Build the color slowly, don't paint it all at once. Note: If you want a tree trunk with a mottled effect, use both black and brown paint. Stencil with one color, let it dry thoroughly, and then highlight with the other color.

5. Set the fabric aside with the stencil in place. Allow the paint to dry thoroughly before removing the stencil. Note: If you're making more than one bag at a time, you may be able to reuse the stencil immediately if you avoid tearing it while removing it.

6. Position the leaf stencil on the stenciled trunk with the leaves just touching the branches. Carefully remove the backing while smoothing the stencil, as you did in step 3.

7. Apply the blue fabric paint: Start stippling the bottom leaves, building the color as deep as you like. As you work toward the top, paint only part of the leaves with the blue. Leave the very top leaves unpainted. Allow the paint to dry thoroughly.

8. Once the blue paint is dry, apply the green. Gently dab the color on the partially stenciled blue leaves for a mottled effect. Paint the top leaves all green.

9. Allow the paint to dry thoroughly, and then remove the leaf stencil. Heat set the paint following the manufacturer's instructions.

MAKE THE BAG

1. Sew the outside of the bag: Place the two pieces of woven fabric together with right sides facing, pin along the sides and bottom, and sew. Use an overcast or tight zigzag stitch on the seam allowance to prevent it from fraying. Do not turn the bag. Repeat with the pieces cut for the lining.

2. Shape the corners: Fold the bag sideways on itself. Match the side seam with the bottom seam until you have a flat corner. Measure approximately 1½ inches (3.8 cm) in from the corner, and draw a line (figure 1). Sew on that line, and then trim the seam. Overcast or zigzag the raw edges. Repeat for the lining. Set the bag and lining aside.

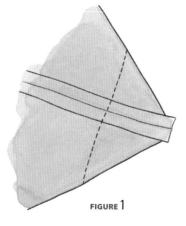

FIGURE 1

3. Make the straps: Pin one of the woven strips to one of the lining strips with right sides together. Sew one of the long sides. Repeat for the other strap. Note: Depending on the fabric you use, you may need to use interfacing to give the straps extra body. Apply the iron-on interfacing to the lining, following the manufacturer's instructions, before pinning the strips together.

4. Turn a strap right side out, and press. Fold the raw edges on the other long side under approximately ¼ inch (6 mm), and press. Pin the folded edges together as you go. Repeat for the other strap.

5. Topstitch ⅛ inch (3 mm) in from both long sides on each of the straps using contrasting or coordinating thread.

6. Turn the bag right side out. Position the straps on the bag with the lining side of the strap facing up. Make sure the ends are an equal distance from the sides on both the front and back. Pin the straps to the top of the bag, aligning the raw edges. Sew the straps as close to the edge of the bag as possible. Turn the bag inside out.

7. Make sure the lining is inside out. Slip it into the bag with right sides facing. Align the side seams, and pin in place. Then pin along the top edge of the bag.

8. Sew around the top of the bag, leaving a 4-inch (10.2 cm) opening for turning. Overcast or zigzag the edges of the seam. Note: Before you sew, make sure the loops of the straps are free of the seam to avoid catching them in the stitches.

9. Put your hand inside the opening, and turn the bag and lining right side out. Tuck the lining into the bag. Press the top of the bag, tucking the raw edges of the opening into the seam allowance as you go.

10. Starting at one of the seams, topstitch ⅛ inch (3 mm) in from the edge around the top of the bag. Use the same thread you used for topstitching the straps in step 5.

APPENDIX

Basic Sewing Kit

Sharp sewing scissors (for fabric)

Craft scissors (for paper)

Rotary cutter and mat

Pinking shears

Sewing machine

Sewing machine needles

Hand-sewing needles

Measuring tape

Transparent ruler

Tailor's chalk or water-soluble
   fabric marker

Needle threader

Seam ripper

Iron and ironing board

Straight pins

Safety and basting pins

Thread

Pencil and paper for making
   templates

Knitting needle
   (for pushing out corners)

Stitch Guide

BACKSTITCH
This simple stitch creates a solid line, so it's great for outlining shapes or creating text.

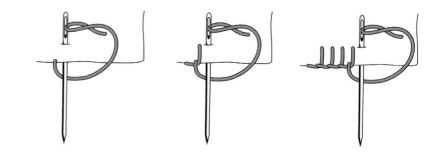

BLANKET STITCH
The blanket stitch is both decorative and functional. Use this stitch to accentuate an edge or to attach an appliqué.

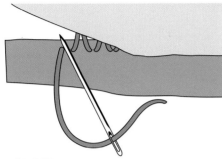

BLINDSTITCH

The blindstitch is perfect for stitching linings to clothing or closing up hems because it remains inconspicuous on either side of the fabric it stitches together. Working from right to left, make a small horizontal stitch that picks up just a thread of one fabric; ¼ inch (.6 cm) to the left, pick up a thread in the other fabric. Repeat, alternating between fabrics.

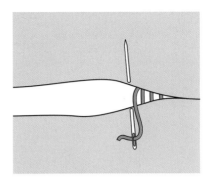

SLIPSTITCH

This stitch is perfect for closing seams. Slip the needle through one end of the open seam to anchor the thread, and then take a small stitch through the fold, pulling the needle through. In the other side of the seam, insert the needle directly opposite the stitch you just made, and take a stitch through the fold. Repeat.

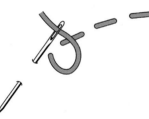

RUNNING STITCH

Make this stitch by weaving the needle through the fabric at evenly spaced intervals.

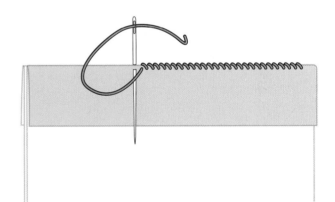

WHIPSTITCH

Also called the overcast stitch, the whipstitch is used to bind edges to prevent raveling or for decorative purposes. Simply stitch over the edge of the fabric.

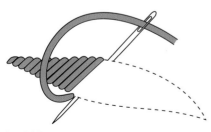

SATIN STITCH

The satin stitch is composed of parallel rows of straight stitches and is often used to fill in an outline.

YARN WEIGHT SYMBOL & CATEGORY NAMES	0 lace	1 super fine	2 fine	3 light	4 medium	5 bulky	6 super bulky
TYPE OF YARNS IN CATEGORY	Fingering 10-count crochet thread	Sock, Fingering, Baby	Sport, Baby	DK, Light Worsted	Worsted, Afghan, Aran	Chunky, Craft, Rug	Bulky, Roving

Source: Craft Yarn Council of America's www.YarnStandards.com

KNITTING ABBREVIATIONS

ABBREVIATION	DESCRIPTION
*	repeat instructions following the single asterisk as directed
BO	bind off
CO	cast on
k or K	knit
p or P	purl
PM	place marker
rnd(s)	round(s)
RS	right side
st(s)	stitch(es)
WS	wrong side

KNITTING NEEDLE SIZE CHART

METRIC (MM)	US	UK/CANADIAN
2.0	0	14
2.25	1	13
2.75	2	12
3.0	—	11
3.25	3	10
3.5	4	—
3.75	5	9
4.0	6	8
4.5	7	7
5.0	8	6
5.5	9	5
6.0	10	4
6.5	10½	3
7.0	—	2
7.5	—	1
8.0	11	0
9.0	13	00
10.0	15	000
12.0	17	—
16.0	19	—
19.0	35	—
25.0	50	—

Goldie

Templates

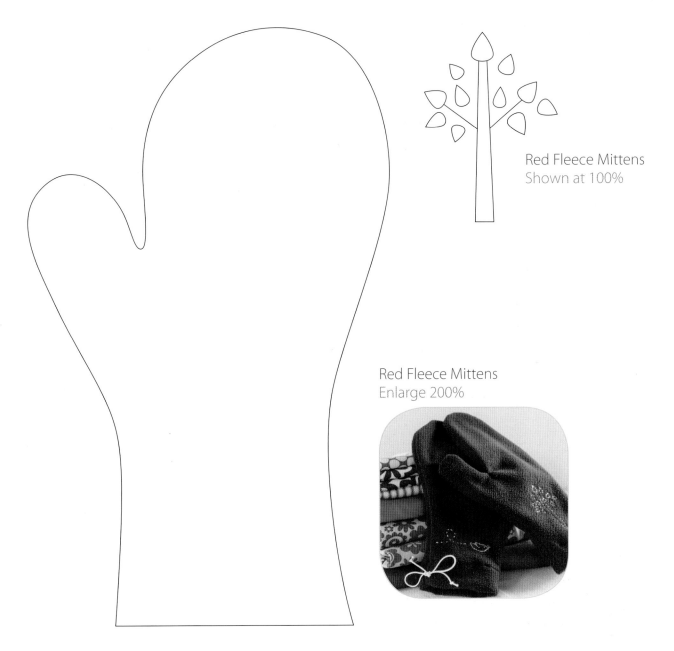

Red Fleece Mittens
Shown at 100%

Red Fleece Mittens
Enlarge 200%

Thank You Cards & Stamp
Enlarge 200%

Stenciled Book Bag
Enlarge 200%

Soft Ball
Enlarge 200%

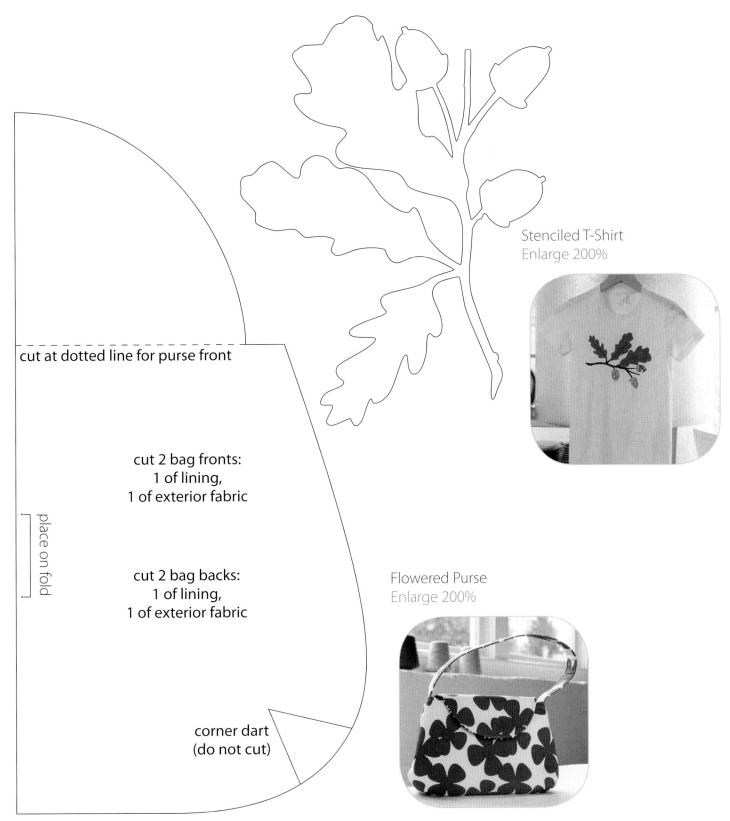

cut at dotted line for purse front

place on fold

cut 2 bag fronts:
1 of lining,
1 of exterior fabric

cut 2 bag backs:
1 of lining,
1 of exterior fabric

corner dart
(do not cut)

Stenciled T-Shirt
Enlarge 200%

Flowered Purse
Enlarge 200%

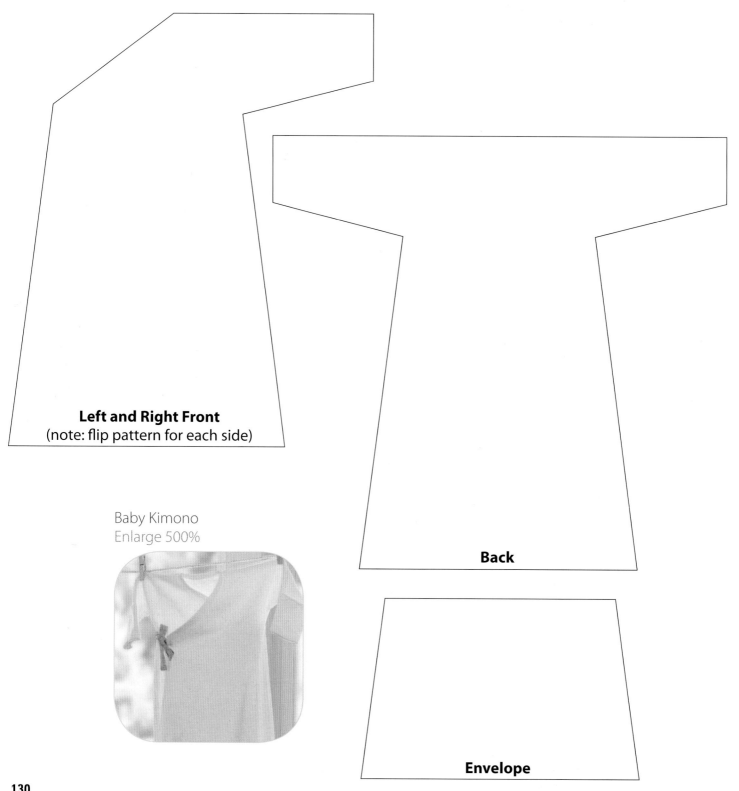

Left and Right Front
(note: flip pattern for each side)

Baby Kimono
Enlarge 500%

Back

Envelope

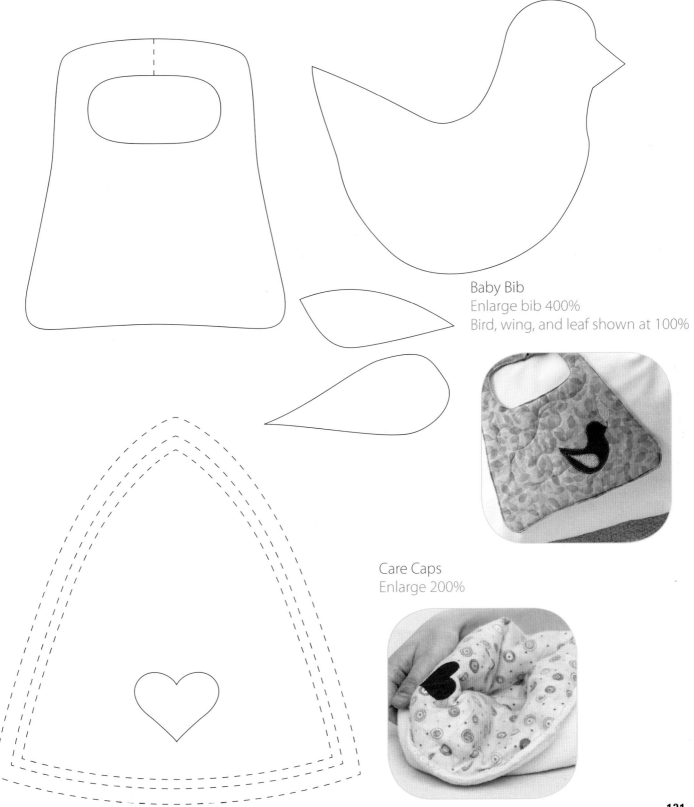

Baby Bib
Enlarge bib 400%
Bird, wing, and leaf shown at 100%

Care Caps
Enlarge 200%

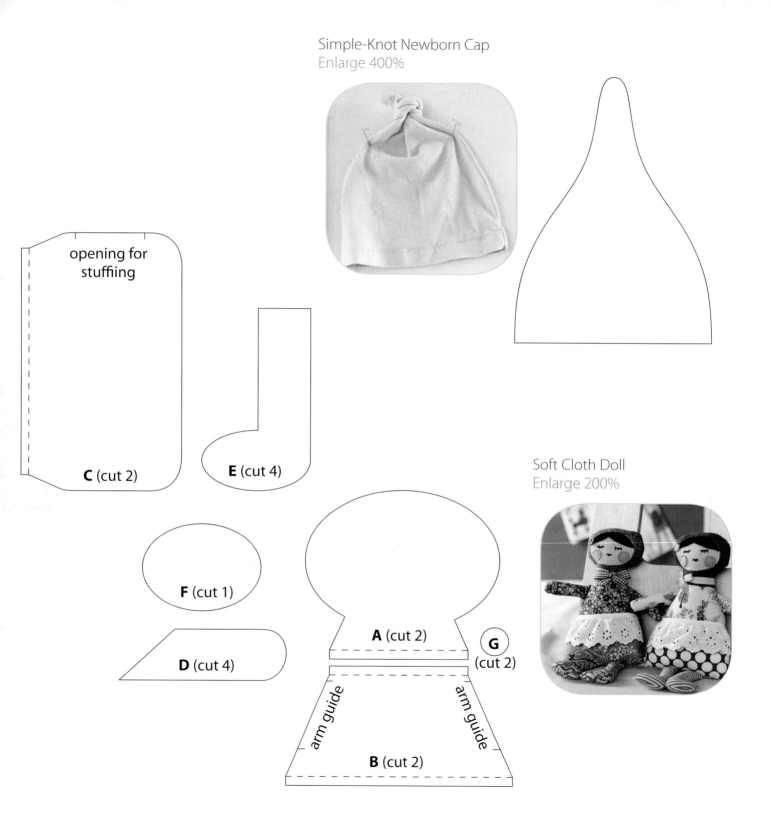

Simple-Knot Newborn Cap
Enlarge 400%

opening for stuffing

C (cut 2)

E (cut 4)

F (cut 1)

D (cut 4)

A (cut 2)

G (cut 2)

arm guide

arm guide

B (cut 2)

Soft Cloth Doll
Enlarge 200%

place
on fold

**pocket
trim
and
yoke
trim**

yoke

place on fold

pocket

place on fold

place on fold

body

Tie-Dyed Snapsuit
Shown at 100%

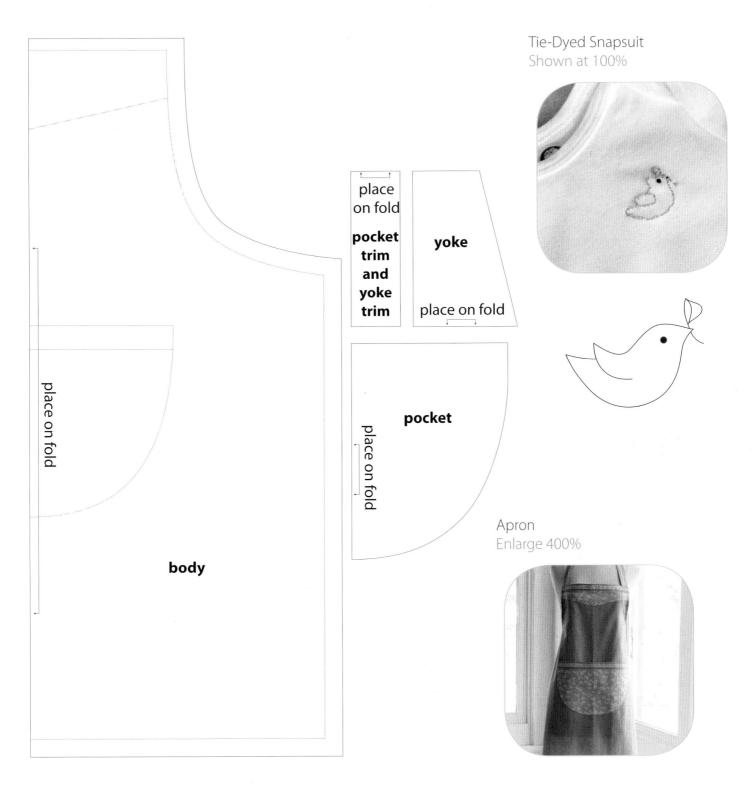

Apron
Enlarge 400%

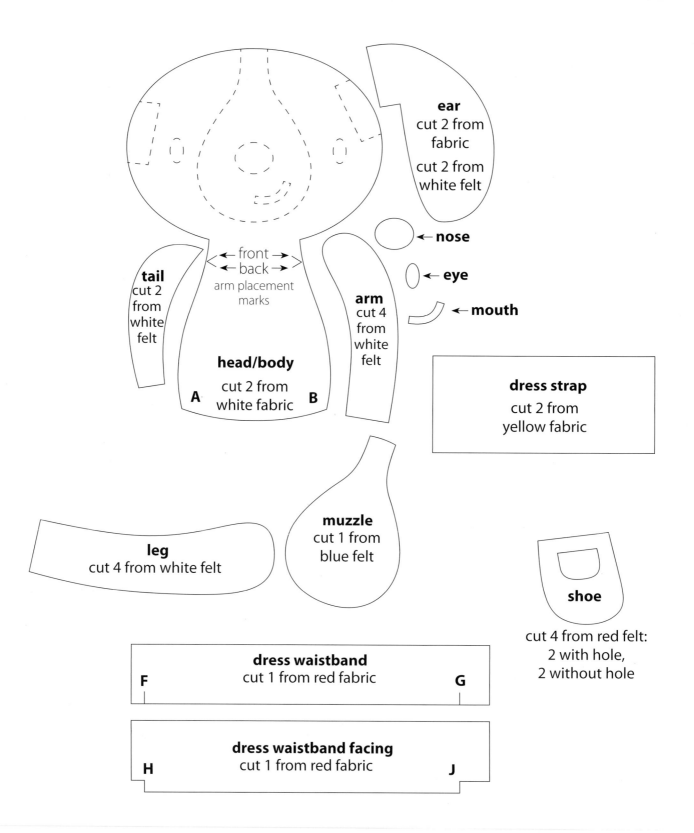

ear
cut 2 from fabric

cut 2 from white felt

← **nose**

← **eye**

← **mouth**

front →
← back
arm placement marks

tail
cut 2 from white felt

arm
cut 4 from white felt

head/body
cut 2 from white fabric

A   B

dress strap
cut 2 from yellow fabric

leg
cut 4 from white felt

muzzle
cut 1 from blue felt

shoe

cut 4 from red felt:
2 with hole,
2 without hole

dress waistband
cut 1 from red fabric

F   G

dress waistband facing
cut 1 from red fabric

H   J

F

D

G

E

Overall
cut 1 from blue
fabric

Overall strap
cut 2 from blue
fabric

XXX

sneaker
cut 4 from
red felt

pocket

cut 1 from
red felt

Overall facing
cut 1 from blue
fabric

Pupkin
Enlarge 200%

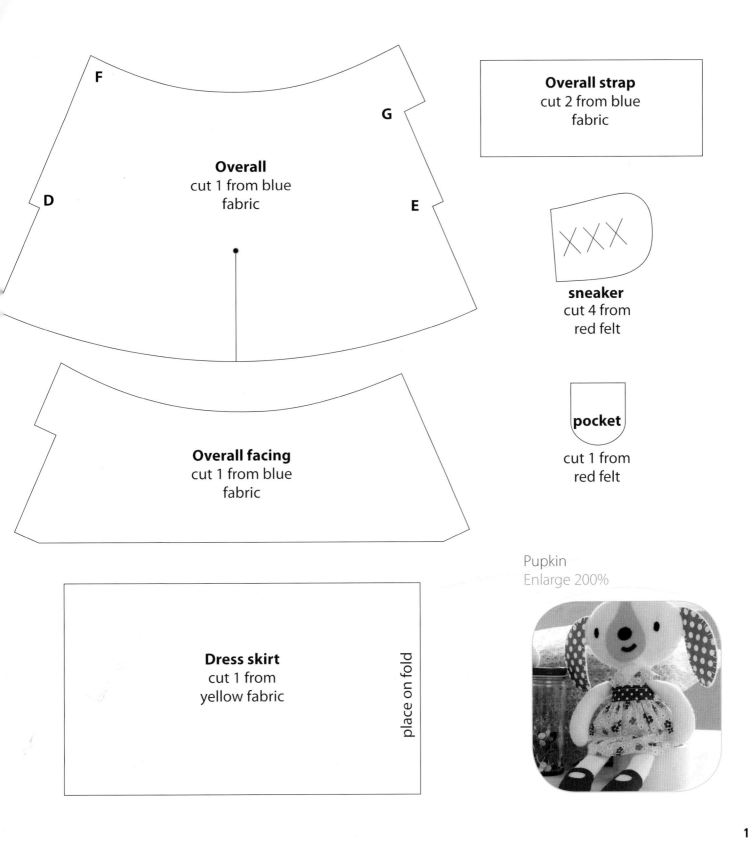

Dress skirt
cut 1 from
yellow fabric

place on fold

About the Designers

All of the designers in *Craft Hope* donated their designs and instructions for this book. It's an inspiring collection of talented artists, and this book is so much richer because of their generosity.

Stefani Austin

Stefani rarely follows project instructions and can't read a pattern to save her life. She leaves the tops off markers, finds the remnants of her craft projects in odd places, constructs castles out of fabric, and—almost daily—finds new and improved ways to use a glue gun. Stefani spends her days trailing after her three imaginative sons. She calls this "homeschooling" and gets away with it. Her nights are spent writing, drawing, sewing, and listening to the tall tales told by her fisherman husband. Stefani writes about her messy, sweet, glitter-speckled life on her blog, www.blueyonderranch.com.

Ellie Beck

A self-taught artist and crafter, Ellie grew up in a creative and nurturing environment, where she was exposed to a wide range of crafts, including weaving, painting, knitting, and sewing. As a young girl, she sewed her brother's tailcoat for a school formal and made clothes for her Barbie dolls. Today her two young children provide inspiration for creative projects and designs. With her husband, Ellie runs a bespoke screen-printing business using organic and sustainable fabrics in Brisbane, Australia. You can read about her crafting and family life at www.petalplum.blogspot.com.

Amanda Carestio

An editorial assistant at Lark Books by day and a serial crafter the rest of the time, Amanda keeps herself busy with various stitching projects, linoleum block prints, and costume-oriented crafting pursuits (especially zombies and pirates). She's the author of *Fa la la la Felt* (Lark Books, 2010). When she's not nose-first in a book, exploring the Blue Ridge, or out scootering the streets, Amanda enjoys spending quality time with her hubby and super-spoiled canines in Asheville, North Carolina. See more of her creative distractions online at www.digsandbean.blogspot.com.

Christina Carleton

Having grown up with a creative mother who sewed everything from sequined prom gowns to auto upholstery, Christina feels sure that nothing is impossible with a sewing machine. She loves the treasure-hunting thrill of a visit to a good thrift store and enjoys sewing clothes for her three girls. Cristina creates unique items from vintage linens. Drawing on her background in advertising design and writing, she blogs about her adventures at www.pinkpicketfence.typepad.com.

Lisa Cox

An avid crafter since childhood, Lisa attributes her passions for sewing, needlecrafts, and quilting to her mother and grandmother, who taught her the basics and encouraged her to develop her own style. There are few crafts that Lisa hasn't dabbled in at one time or another! She works as an occupational therapist by day and crafts at night. Lisa has published recipes and crafts in *Du Jour* (2008); *Pretty Little Presents* (Lark Books, 2009); *Sweet Nothings* (Lark Books, 2009); and *Silver Magazine*. Lisa lives in a coastal suburb of Perth, Australia, with her husband, David, and their children, Brenton and Sarah. Lisa and Sarah collaborate on a popular blog, *A Spoonful of Sugar* (www.spoonfullofsugargirls.blogspot.com), where readers can follow their crafting and baking adventures.

Maya Donenfeld

Maya lives with her husband and two children in upstate New York, where she spends her days creating and re-purposing in her old farmhouse. Maya's biggest inspirations come from her children and her rural surroundings. She's also inspired by the contents of her recycling bins. Maya shares ideas for creative parenting and green living on her blog, *maya*made* (www.mayamade.com.).

Malka Dubrawsky

Malka was introduced to art in the eighth grade, and she hasn't been the same since. She graduated from college with a BFA in studio art and spent many years as a fiber artist. Her work has been featured in a number of prestigious shows and publications, including Quilt National, Quilt Visions, and *Fiberarts: Design Book 7*. Malka's current focus is making quilts, pillows, and other sundries from her own hand-dyed and patterned fabric. Her creations are sold at her online store, www.stitchindye.etsy.com. Malka writes and designs patterns and has been published in *Quilting Arts Magazine, Stitch*, and several books, including *Sweater Surgery* and *Quilts! Baby* (Lark Books, 2009). Her own book, *Color Your Cloth: A Quilter's Guide to Dyeing and Patterning Fabric*, was published by Lark Books in 2009.

Molly Dunham

Molly has been crafting and creating since grade school. She enjoys knitting, crocheting, sewing, embroidery, cooking, gardening, and photography. In life and in craft, she makes up patterns as she goes along and is rarely surprised (but often delighted) when things don't turn out as planned. Molly lives in the foothills of the Sierra Nevada with her husband, two children, a free-range bunny, and a flock of chickens. Visit her online at www.foothillhomecompanion.blogspot.com.

Céline Dupuy

Céline is the designer of the Mlle Kou easy patterns. Well known for her innovative sewing ideas, she creates stylish designs that are frequently featured in the pages of *Marie Claire Idées*. Céline is the author of the books *Make Your Own Handbags* and *Simple Sewing with a French Twist*. Since the birth of her son, Edgar, she splits her time between Paris and Poitiers, France. Her websites are www.celinedupuy.com and www.mllekou.com.

Cathie Filian

Cathie is an Emmy-nominated television host, lifestyle expert, and designer. She is the creator, producer, and co-host of the HGTV and DIY lifestyle shows *Creative Juice* and *Witch Crafts*. Cathie has also appeared on the Discovery Channel and the Food Network. She is the author of *101 Snappy Fashions* (Lark Books, 2010), *Bow Wow WOW!* (Lark Books, 2008), and *Creative Juice—45 Re-Crafting Projects*. Before stepping in front of the camera, Cathie worked behind the scenes in the movie industry, creating costumes for the films *Rushmore, Twister, Heartbreakers*, and *Vanilla Sky*. Cathie lives in Los Angeles with her husband, Eddie, and their dog Max. Visit her online at www.cathiefilian.com.

Wendi Gratz

Wendi lives with her family and her sewing machine in western North Carolina. In high school she skipped home ec in favor of wood and metal shop, and she didn't learn to use a sewing machine until college. Now she makes fun clothes, funky dolls, and all kinds of quilts. Wendi is the author of *Absolutely A-Line* (Lark Books, 2009), and she's published work in *Simple Contemporary Quilts* (Lark Books, 2010), *Sweet Booties* (Lark Books, 2009), *You Lucky Dog* (Lark Books, 2009), and many of the *Pretty Little* series (Lark Books). You can see her work at www.wendigratz.com.

Betsy Greer

Betsy writes about the intersection of craft and activism at www.craftivism.com. Her book, *Knitting for Good!*, was published by Shambhala Publications in November 2008. She crafts, writes, and drinks entirely too much coffee in North Carolina.

Jenny B Harris

Jenny has been making stuff since she was a wee thing. Whether she's illustrating children's books, designing patterns, or stitching toys, Jenny thinks that a day spent in the studio is a great day. She lives and works in a creatively decorated home in Dallas, Texas (which is heroically tolerated by her architect husband). Read about her craft adventures via her blog, www.allsorts.typepad.com.

Vickie Howell

Mother, designer, author, and crafty spokesperson, Vickie served as host and creative consultant for the television show *Knitty Gritty* for eight seasons. She has also served as co-host of the DIY Network's *Stylelicious* and as needle arts host for myLifetime.com's CRAFTED series. Vickie writes a celebrity column for Knit.1 Magazine, an online craft column for PBS Parents, and is a regular contributor to Craftzine.com. Vickie has produced several best-selling craft books, including her most recent, *Craft Corps* (Lark Books, 2010). For more information on Vickie and her projects, visit www.vickiehowell.com.

Rebecca Ittner

Rebecca was raised in California in a family that encouraged creativity. Instead of watching television, she and her siblings played with clay, drew, painted with watercolors, and generally made their own fun. An editor, photo-stylist, and craft enthusiast, Rebecca is the author of *Soapmaking the Natural Way* (Lark Books, 2010) and *Candlemaking the Natural Way* (Lark Books, 2010). To see more of Rebecca's work, visit www.rebeccaittner.etsy.com or www.livelovecraft.com.

Rebeka Lambert

Beki lives with her husband and three children on the outskirts of Baton Rouge, Louisiana. She inherited her love of sewing from her mother and grandmother. She enjoys creating bags, purses, quilts, and sweet little dresses for her daughters. Although she put crafting on hold during her first years as a mother, Beki is back at it thanks in part to the discovery of craft blogs. The daily feedback and sharing of ideas through blogging keeps her inspired. Beki has contributed to Lark Books' *Pretty Little* series, with projects featured in *Pretty Little Potholders* (Lark Books, 2008), *Pretty Little Patchwork* (Lark Books, 2008), and *Pretty Little Purses and Pouches* (Lark Books, 2008). Visit her online at www.artsycraftybabe.typepad.com and www.artsycraftybabe.etsy.com.

Kathy Mack

Kathy lives on Bainbridge Island, Washington, with two beautiful daughters and a husband who encourages her wacky ideas. Kathy has been sewing since she was six, when her grandmother taught her the basics. Inspired by the chaotic pace of family life, she enjoys designing accessories, handbags, and quilts that bring color, joy, function, and beauty to everyday living. Kathy splits her day between caring for her kids, running her sewing pattern business, www.PinkChalkStudio.com, and tending her online fabric store, www.PinkChalkFabrics.com. In her spare time she writes about her crafty adventures at www.pinkchalkstudio.com/blog.

Kaari Meng

Kaari is the owner of French General, a small home interior shop in Hollywood, California. The shop specializes in 18th-century French hemp sheets and offers vintage craft classes. The author of *The French-Inspired Home* (Lark Books, 2006) and *Home Sewn*, Kaari spends her summers in France shopping for vintage wares. She and her Basque husband have a beautiful little girl.

Manda McGrory

Following an unusual career path that included running away with the circus, training as a carpenter, and working as a bank manager, Manda McGrory discovered her true passion for all things textile in 2005, when she was expecting her first daughter. Within a year, Manda started her own company, TreeFall Designs, and gained a large readership for her craft blog of the same name. Her career has continued to grow, and Manda now publishes her sewing patterns worldwide. You can find out more about her at www.treefalldesigns.com.

Jhoanna Monte

Jhoanna lives in Melbourne, Australia, with her two daughters. She produces a variety of craft projects, soft toys, and accessories under the label One Red Robin. Jhoanna has participated in a number of plush art exhibitions, including a solo show in Hong Kong, and her creations have found new homes with customers around the world. In November 2008, Jhoanna launched her own line of soft-toy sewing patterns in partnership with Pattern Press. By day, she works as an IT analyst and at night, she works in her small home studio. Jhoanna's sewing projects have been published in Australia's premiere craft magazines. Her website is www.oneredrobin.com.

Aimee Ray

Aimee has been making things from paper, fabric, and clay for as long as she can remember. She is the author of the bestselling book *Doodle-Stitching* (Lark Books, 2007), a collection of contemporary embroidery designs, and its sequel, *Doodle Stitching: The Motif Collection* (Lark Books, 2010). She has contributed to many Lark titles. To see more of her work, visit www.dreamfollow.com.

Eren Hays San Pedro

In 2004 Eren went to Nicaragua with ORPHANetwork and has since continued to visit the staff and children of the orphanages located there. Her first doll project for the Craft Hope website combined her passions for outreach and crafts. The mother of three very active little boys, Eren learned to sew and crochet from the extremely talented women in her family. Find out more about her by visiting her blog at www.vintagechica.typepad.com.

Amanda Blake Soule

Amanda lives in coastal Maine with her four young children and husband. She shares her family's creative adventures on her daily blog, www.SouleMama.com. Amanda is the author of *The Creative Family: How to Encourage Imagination and Nurture Family Connections*, and *Handmade Home: Simple Ways to Repurpose Old Materials into New Family Treasures.*

Blair Stocker

Blair has been making things since she was a child in North Carolina, where she spent afternoons with her grandmother learning to sew and knit. Although she lives with her husband and two kids, Blair carves out time to sew, knit, quilt, cook, and create things that make her Seattle, Washington, house feel like home. She contributes regularly to craft books and publications. Blair writes about what she makes—as well as what she hopes to make—on her blog, *Wise Craft*. Visit her online at www.blairpeter.typepad.com.

Amanda Swan

Mom by day and seamstress by night, Amanda juggles a hectic household that includes four young children with the help of her husband, Christopher. At night, Amanda's laundry room is transformed into a workstation, where she designs and creates colorful travel accessories, blankets, and more. Read her "Many Roles of Mom" blog at www.sygnetcreations.blogspot.com, or visit her store at www.sygnetcreations.etsy.com.

Beth Sweet

Beth comes from a long line of creative women, though that line falls into two camps: the grandmas and great-grandmas who taught home ec and used patterns religiously, and the mom and aunts who whole-heartedly applaud the "wing-it" approach to crafting. Beth likes to keep things interesting by winging it with cupcake experiments, portable summer herb gardens, and adventures with her wiggly dog in Asheville, North Carolina.

Susan Wasinger

Susan learned to sew from her couture-trained Swiss grandmother at the age of four. She's sewn for everything from trade shows to modern dance performances and is undaunted by the prospect of stitching unusual projects on her home machine. In addition to clothing and decor, Wasinger designs houses and a variety of products. A regular contributor to craft books and magazines, she's been featured in *Metropolitan Home, Stitch, Natural Home,* and *Piecework*. She has also appeared on HGTV. Susan is the author of *Eco Craft* (Lark Books, 2009) and *The Feisty Stitcher* (Lark Books, 2010). She also served as photographer and designer for *Fa la la la Felt* (Lark Books, 2010). Wasinger lives in Boulder, Colorado, with her Grammy Award-winning husband, two feisty children, and a 120-pound dog.

Dana Willard

When Dana's children go to sleep at night, the countdown begins. Sewing projects, refashioning ideas, blogging, photo tweaking, hairclip stitching, and late-night cookie baking often keep Dana up till the early hours of the morning. Thanks to the presence of her children—two adorable, live-in models—Dana often creates sewing projects for youngsters. In addition to sewing, she enjoys working on photo shoots because they provide exciting ways to showcase creative ideas. Visit her online at www.dana-made-it.com.

Rebekah Williams

Rebekah's obsession with sewing and crafting began harmlessly enough as a fabric fixation. These days, many of the drawers, bags, suitcases, and dressers in her house are brimming—no, bursting (at the seams!)—with fabric. In the daytime, Rebekah enjoys the adventure of raising two preschoolers and hanging out with her husband, Nathan. In the wee hours, she can be found at her sewing machine, eagerly transforming fabrics into original creations. Read more about her crafting, parenting, and photography pursuits at www.yeebird.blogspot.com.

Geninne D. Zlatkis

An artist, illustrator, and graphic designer, Geninne lives above a mountain forest near Mexico City with her husband, Manolo, their two creative boys, and a Border Collie named Turbo. Born in New York, Geninne moved around often as a child, living in seven different countries in South America. She studied architecture in Chile before earning a degree as a graphic artist in Mexico. Today she works in a variety of media, including watercolor, ink, and pencil. Geninne loves to sew, embroider, and carve stamps by hand. She sells prints of her watercolors at her online Etsy Shop, www.geninne.etsy.com. Her blog is www.geninne.com.

About the Author

Jade Sims lives just outside Austin, Texas, in the Hill Country with her patient husband and three rambunctious children. She spends her days playing hide-n-seek, finger painting, cleaning up glitter, and changing diapers, while running the Craft Hope website (www.crafthope.com) from her laptop. She blogs about her life at www.chikaustin.com.

Acknowledgments

Craft Hope would not exist without the support of the blogging community that joined in, contributed, and spread the word. To everyone around the world who has become a part of Craft Hope—thank you!

The incredibly talented designers featured in this book graciously donated their patterns to Craft Hope. Thank you for your artistry, time, and belief in the significance of this project.

A warm thank you goes to Kristen Roedner of Faux-Toes Photography for taking wonderful pictures of my family, Eric Carroll of Visual Notion for the Craft Hope logo, and my husband, Miles Sims, for creating the Craft Hope website and design.

A lifetime of thanks to my family—Miles, Makena, Keegan, and Chloe—who supported me and waited patiently for me to finish "one last thing," so I could make their peanut butter and jelly sandwiches. To my husband, Miles, who understood my vision for Craft Hope and made it appear on the world wide web. To Makena and Keegan, who paraded in costumes in circles around me while I worked. To Chloe, my baby, who patiently bounced on my knee while I worked on the computer.

I would like to thank the incredible team at Lark Crafts for their vision and hand-holding throughout this process. I am eternally grateful to Kathy Sheldon, my editor and friend, who ever so patiently guided me through this process and helped to maintain the integrity of my vision for Craft Hope. She trusted me with this incredible opportunity. Special thanks to Beth Sweet, my editorial assistant, for keeping me on task and moving forward when my mind tended to wander, and Carol Morse, junior designer, for saving the day. Thanks also to Kristi Pfeffer, Dana Irwin, Lana Lê, Orrin Lundgren, Lynne Harty, and Pamela Norman for their creative support and inspiration.

And a special thanks to Amy Butler and Heather Bailey for donating fabric for projects in the book and to help Hearts in Unity's sewing co-op in Tanzania.

A big thanks to everyone who made Craft Hope and this book possible. Spread a little hope!

Photo Credits

We're able to show you the work these charities do and the people they serve because of the generosity of many photographers—some professionals, some anonymous volunteers around the world with digital cameras, and some Craft Hope members who snapped their handmade donations before sending them on their way. Our deepest gratitude to everyone who provided images for the book.

Special thanks to Kristen Roedner of www.faux-toes.com (Jade and family: pages 6 and 142); Jeannie Hampton (girls in their pillowcase dresses, back cover and pages 7, 15, and 17); Eren Hays San Pedro (children with soft dolls, front cover and pages 7, 10, and 31); Tracy Chapman (hands holding doll, page 7); Stephanie TeSlaa of www.miraclesphotography.com (children with Margaret's Hope Chest quilts, front cover, pages 8, 11, and 45); Patricia Conesa (box of sock monkeys, page 8); Timothy Bouldry of www.timothybouldry.com (baby in La Chureca, pages 14 and 109); Scott Andre (child with mittens, pages 14 and 55); Jenny B Harris (pupkin, page 96), and Susan Wasinger of www.lostangelstudios.com (seedballs and flowers, pages 106 and 107).

Index